W9-CCJ-091

PROPERTY OF
LOUISVILLE PUBLIC LIBRARY

COOL CAREERS WITHOUT COLLEGE FOR
PEOPLE
WHO LOVE
MANGA, COMICS,
AND ANIMATION

COOL CAREERS WITHOUT COLLEGE FOR
PEOPLE
WHO LOVE
MANGA, COMICS,
AND ANIMATION

SHERRI GLASS
AND JIM WENTZEL

The Rosen Publishing Group, Inc., New York

y
741.5
GLA

Published in 2007 by The Rosen Publishing Group, Inc.
29 East 21st Street, New York, NY 10010

Copyright © 2007 by The Rosen Publishing Group, Inc.

First Edition

All rights reserved. No part of this book may be reproduced in any form without permission in writing from the publisher, except by a reviewer.

Library of Congress Cataloging-in-Publication Data

Glass, Sherri.
Cool careers without college for people who love manga, comics, and animation/Sherri Glass and Jim Wentzel.—1st ed.
    p. cm.—(Cool careers without college)
Includes index.
ISBN 1-4042-0754-6 (library binding)
1. Animated films—Vocational guidance. 2. Comic books, strips, etc.—Vocational guidance. I. Wentzel, Jim, 1968– II. Title. III. Series.

NC1765.G55 2006
741.5023'73—dc22

2005033231

Manufactured in the United States of America

CONTENTS

INTRODUCTION

If you have picked up this book, you are most likely the kind of person who has spent a lot of time doodling on napkins, filling sketchbooks with your own drawings, or watching cartoons beginning at a very young age. Perhaps you are a big fan of comics, and you have loved *Batman*, *Spider-Man*, or *Peanuts* since you were a child. Maybe more recently you have become interested in Japanese-style comics—known as manga—and would like to learn how to create those distinctive drawings yourself.

Whatever your particular interests and enthusiasms, you are probably beginning to wonder if you can earn a living by indulging your passion for comics and animation. You are certainly not alone. Your imagination has been captured by the magic of line art. Dynamic, drama-packed panels on a comic's page or animated images on a movie or TV screen speak to you in ways that many other visual and literary art forms do not.

Thanks in part to highly successful big-budget animated films like *The Incredibles* and *Shrek*, TV shows like *The Simpsons* and *Family Guy*, and film adaptations of popular graphic fiction like *Sin City* and *Ghost World*, comics and animation have recently enjoyed widespread acceptance by the mainstream not witnessed since comics' golden age, in the late 1930s. This was the era when Superman first appeared on newsstands in *Action Comics* #1, sparking the superhero craze in the world of comic books. You are most likely someone who has not only seen these shows and films and read the source material, but possibly can name all of the characters, recite dialogue, identify subtle shifts in the plot, note weaknesses in the line art or motion graphics, or pinpoint sequences that could have been improved with better voice characterization. If you feel you have some potential talent in these areas and would like to make a living from this talent, then this book will help set you on that path.

The habit of doodling and sketching in notebooks can lead to a career in comics and animation. Scott Ziolko, creator of the comic book series *Test-Tube*, sketches one of his characters, Lewis, above. Ziolko began creating the characters in this series while working as a restaurant cook.

Among the most obvious career directions for someone with an interest in graphic storytelling are the numerous jobs available in the comic book industry. From superhero comics (like *The Fantastic Four* and *Batman*) to manga from Japan (like *Shaman King*), there are many choices. We will profile some of the key roles in the production process that result in the sales of finished copies of comic books and manga and offer some helpful entry points for you to begin your job search in your preferred segment of these industries.

Similarly, within the field of animation, we will look at several careers that offer creative opportunities and a wide range of challenges. The animation process can range from true do-it-yourself productions created on a personal computer to big-budget, feature-length Hollywood studio films that can involve literally hundreds of people laboring behind the scenes on specialized animation tasks. As in any highly competitive field that employs relatively few people, it can take a lot of work and passion to separate yourself from other interested job seekers and get your foot in the door, but we will recommend ways for you to get a solid start.

Before you begin your job search, you might want to ask yourself a few questions: What kind of artist do you want to be? What sort of message do you want to bring to your readers or viewers? How do you most like to express yourself? What graphic art brings you the most happiness and satisfaction? Which artists do you most admire? Remember as you read this book that you should try to choose a career that makes you happy and helps you realize your professional goals at the same time. This is the best path for long-term enjoyment of your field of choice.

COMICS

What do we mean by the term "comics"? Comics can take several forms, from daily newspaper strips like *Doonesbury* and comic books we see on newsstands and in bookstores, like the recent *Justice*, to elaborate graphic novels like Art Spiegelman's *Maus*. At their most basic level, comics are a collection of illustrated panels laid out on a page with the intention of telling a linear story. They are typically rendered

The abundant offerings of a typical comic store appears above. Many stores display their comics by publisher and genre. The shelves of this store group together DC's superhero comics—such as *Justice League of America*, *Smallville*, and *Superman (above left)*—while the rear rack displays graphic novels. The wall between these two groupings contains a selection of Marvel titles, including *Spider-Man*, *The Fantastic Four*, and *Wolverine* (of the X-Men).

with black inked lines and are often colored for a more vivid, dramatic, or realistic effect. Comics have the ability to use dynamic and evocative imagery to enhance a written story, creating a visual experience that rivals film in its sense of movement, excitement, mood, and action.

Comic books have their origins in political cartoons, late-nineteenth-century comic strips, and science fiction

The Yellow Kid

The Yellow Kid, of the late-nineteenth-century *Hogan's Alley* comic strip, was the first successful comic strip character. The character—a street urchin who mocked New York's upper classes—was named after the tallow-colored gown he wore. The character eventually achieved a popularity so widespread that he actually increased the sales of newspapers carrying the strip. In addition to belonging to the first color comic strip, the Yellow Kid was also among the first comic characters to be merchandised profitably. The Yellow Kid appeared in newspapers between 1895 and 1898, and his creator, R. F. Outcault (who went on to create the character Buster Brown), deserves enormous credit for establishing the comic strip as a legitimate medium.

William Paquet *(above)* often works for DC Comics, creating models of reproduction figures based on DC characters that are sold in comic shops and other stores nationwide. In the above photograph, he is working on a model of Nosferatu, the very first movie vampire who appeared in F. W. Murnau's 1922 film *Nosferatu*. Paquet's company, Paquet Film Works, is run from his basement in Staunton, Virginia.

stories of the 1920s. They came into their own in the 1930s with the appearance of *Superman* and *Batman*. Over the years, many of these early "superhero" titles spawned other comic series and, in some cases, big-budget, live-action movies. Today, an enormous industry has grown up around the merchandising of comic characters, including toys, video games, and action figures. If you consider the amount of merchandise made available as tie-ins to a film like *Spider-Man 2*—from pajamas to plastic action figures given away

with meals at fast-food restaurants—these characters have a powerful impact on popular culture.

Over time, comic production has become more and more wide open as a field. Many artists are publishing their own work independent of the major publishers. In turn, they are inspiring other artists to strike out on their own. There are more work tools and career avenues open to the aspiring comic author than ever before. Even though it can take a lot of practice and discipline to draw as well as the established artists, many of the great comic artists of the past and present did not receive a college degree or formal art school training. Instead, they achieved success through their own creative vision, tireless persistence, and hard work. So take your own ideas for a story and consider crafting them into a reality.

COMIC BOOK SCRIPTWRITER

If you find yourself more interested in the verbal rather than visual story-telling of a comic strip or comic book, then you may want to try your hand at writing comic scripts. Scriptwriters, among their many duties, write all of the dialogue for the comic, which lends color, drama, humor, and meaning to the story. Writers develop the plot, establish the narrative flow, and set the

Robert Kirkman *(above)* is a comic book writer from Lexington, Kentucky. Arrayed below him are several of the comic books he has written. Kirkman began as a comic book reader and fan. With no college education, he got a warehouse job after high school. Eventually, he began writing and self-publishing his own comic books. He is now published by Image Comics.

tone. They describe in detail all of the various "shots"—the action and images contained in each panel of the comic strip or comic book. Much as a movie script details the action that the camera will film, a comic book script describes in words the flow of events in the panels that will appear on the printed page. It is a writer's job to show, not simply tell.

As a comic scriptwriter, you will hand off your finished script to the penciller, who will begin translating your written dialogue, directions, and ideas into visual form in a series of panels. Communicating your ideas is important, but there is no one right way of doing it. Certain writers prefer to hand off full scripts with lots of specific directions, leaving very little to the penciller's creative imagination. For example, some scripts may contain specifics like panel size and detailed captions explaining elaborate "camera shots" (descriptions of the way characters should fill a panel and what angle they should be seen from). Other writers prefer to communicate just the basic plot and dialogue and give the penciller full creative reign to expand the story visually as he or she sees fit.

Among the most successful comic publishers is Marvel Comics. Much of its success has been based on the creation of its so-called Marvel Universe. Its "universe" is a collection of characters who have common historical and geographic reference points that unite them. Because they

Neil Gaiman is perhaps one of the world's best known and most respected graphic novelists. He has written dozens of comics and graphic novels for several publishers, including DC, for whom he wrote the extremely popular *Sandman* series. *The Sandman* is often credited with raising the cultural and literary profile of the comic genre. Gaiman has worked as a journalist and has written songs, poems, television series, screenplays, and several novels, including 2005's best seller *Anansi Boys*. Gaiman appears opposite signing copies of the novel. Though English, Gaiman now lives with his wife and children in Minnesota.

inhabit the same imaginative universe, one character often makes a guest appearance in another character's comic, without there being any jarring conflict of tone or narrative style. This is something you may want to consider in creating your own comics—a well-defined and expandable world for the characters to inhabit and in which to develop, and possibly be joined by additional characters as time goes by.

Some writers are also handy artists and prefer to draw (and in some cases ink and color) their own scripts rather than hand them off to a penciller, inker, and colorist. Among the most famous of these is Frank Miller, who authored *Sin City* and *The Dark Knight Returns*, both well-known comic series. Many artists publish their work through independent publishers, earning them the moniker "underground cartoonists." These artists generally reach a smaller audience, but many achieve lasting cult fame. Among the most famous of these artists are Robert Crumb *(Zap Comics, Fritz the Cat)*, Jeff Smith *(Bone)*, and Art Spiegelman *(Maus)*.

Probably the most famous comic writer of all is Stan Lee, who helped create Marvel Comics and make it the household name it is today. At Marvel, he cocreated *Spider-Man*, *The Fantastic Four*, *The Incredible Hulk*, *The X-Men*, and *Daredevil*. While admittedly not an artist, Lee's contribution to comics is huge. His career is a tribute to the fact that even if you cannot draw, there can be a vital and creative role for you to play in the comic industry.

Education and Training

While it is not required that you have an English degree to become a writer, it will help to have strong language and grammar skills. A good writer should be familiar with a wide range of comics and artists past and present, and read widely in the medium. A solid grounding in literature, drama, history, mythology, folklore, and film will also provide you with further creative stimulation and inspiration.

Visit your local comic shop and seek out the classics in the various comic genres, from old newspaper strips to newer independent comic artists. Use the Internet to research new artists and their work, and read interviews with comic authors to learn about their techniques. Take writing classes and share your work with other writers. Practice writing your own stories, both short stories and more elaborate novellas, and decide which method suits you best. Network with other writers in online forums. Don't limit yourself to comics—read plays, film scripts, and novels. It is important to steep yourself thoroughly in the craft of writing, not just comic writing. The best way to do that is to read, and read widely.

Most comic books average twenty-two pages, and most editors will prefer that a complete script be submitted. Be sure to refer to the publishers' Web sites for their specific submission guidelines, and become familiar with them. Some publishers may not accept unsolicited submissions. DC Comics runs a DC Talent Search at designated comic

Students watch their drawing instructor demonstrate a particular technique in an art class at Spokane Falls Community College in Spokane, Washington. Community and technical colleges often offer art classes to the public. Usually you do not have to have yet graduated from high school or be enrolled in a degree program to take these courses.

conventions. Attending conventions is one of the smartest ways to make yourself known. There is no better way to make contacts, circulate your work, get feedback, and perhaps even chat with editors.

You should become familiar with basic word processing software like Microsoft Word, as it will make it easier and quicker to share your work electronically with other artists. Stay confident even in the face of rejection; often it can take a lot of time to get your script into an editor's hands and many rejection letters before you receive an offer. You might want to create a basic Web site to post some of your work so that if publishers request it, you can simply send them your URL.

Outlook

Comic book script writing is an ideal career for writers of all kinds who want to express themselves more visually than straightforward prose or poetry allows. With the Pulitzer Prize–winning *Maus* graphic novel published in 1986 and the recent spate of live-action films based on original comics (*Spider-Man and Spider-Man 2*, *Batman Begins*, *Daredevil*, *American Splendor*, and *Sin City*), comic books and comic art are currently very much in the public eye. Marvel comics editor-in-chief Joe Quesada recently noted in an interview with popthought.com, "The one thing that I believe in is the knowledge that no matter what the medium, whether it be movies, TV, books, comic books, or video games, it all starts with one important thing—great writing. Writers are the key to success."

Salary

Some top writers can make up to $100,000 a year writing a few ongoing titles (such as the superhero comics). This is not the norm, though. You will typically have to work your way up the ladder slowly and get paid by the page. Typical page rates for beginners are $40 to $60, and, once you have more experience under your belt, $80 to $100.

FOR MORE INFORMATION

ORGANIZATIONS

Comic-Con International
P.O. Box 128458
San Diego, CA 92112-8458
(619) 491-2475
Web site: http://www.comic-con.org
   Comic-Con International is a nonprofit educational organization dedicated to creating awareness of and appreciation for comics and related popular art forms, primarily through the presentation of conventions and events that celebrate the historic and ongoing contribution of comics to art and culture.

Dark Horse Comics
10956 S.E. Main Street
Milwaukie, OR 97222
(503) 652-8815
Web site: http://www.darkhorse.com
   Dark Horse Comics is the third-largest comic book publisher in the United States and is recognized as the world's leading publisher of licensed comic material. It has published comics from top talent like Frank Miller, Mike Mignola, Stan Sakai, Sergio Aragonés, Neil Gaiman, and Will Eisner. Its highly successful line of comics based on popular properties includes *Star Wars*, *Buffy the Vampire Slayer*, *Aliens*, *Conan*, and, most recently, *The Incredibles*.

Drawn & Quarterly
P.O. Box 48056
Montreal, Quebec, Canada H2V4S8
Web site: http://www.drawnandquarterly.com

One of the most influential art and literary comic publishers in North America.

Fantagraphics Books
7563 Lake City Way NE
Seattle, WA 98115
(800) 657-1100
Web site: http://www.fantagraphics.com
Fantagraphics Books is one of the premier independent comic publishers. Its Web site keeps you up-to-date on what is happening in the underground comic industry and will be a great reference for keeping tabs on the latest and greatest writers, artists, and their work.

Marvel Entertainment, Inc.
417 Fifth Avenue
New York, NY 10016
Web site: http://www.marvel.com
Publisher of *Spider-Man*, *The X-Men*, *Captain America*, *The Fantastic Four*, and *The Avengers*, among many others.

WEB SITES

COMICON.com: Virtual Comics Convention
http://www.comicon.com
Official Web site for COMICON, the world's biggest comic convention.

Creating Comics
http://www.members.shaw.ca/creatingcomics
Excellent collection of links to all kinds of resources for aspiring comic writers.

Down the Tubes: Breaking into Comics Guide
http://www.downthetubes.net/writing_comics/index.html

Essay by John Freeman, former Marvel UK editor, entitled "Breaking into Comics." Freeman advises artists to "self-publish if you can afford it" and to "be prepared to revise your storyline" if an editor asks you to.

Idea Tracker
http://www.intellectusenterprises.com/IdeaTracker.html
Idea Tracker software is a helpful tool for organizing your comic ideas.

Interview with Joe Quesada, Marvel Comics' editor-in-chief
http://popthought.com/display_column.asp?DAID=430

Microsoft Word blank template documents for comic book scripts
http://ourworld.compuserve.com/homepages/sgerber/TEMPLATS.htm

Submission guidelines for Dark Horse Comics
http://www.darkhorse.com/company/submissions.php

Submission guidelines for Drawn & Quarterly
http://www.drawnandquarterly.com/aboutSubmission.php

Wikipedia's "Marvel Comics" entry
http://en.wikipedia.org/wiki/Marvel_Comics
An introduction to one of the most famous and influential comic companies in the world.

BOOKS

Caputo, Tony C. *How to Self-Publish Your Own Comic Book: The Complete Resource Guide to the Business, Production, Distribution, Marketing and Promotion of Comic Books.* New York, NY: Watson-Guptill Publications, 1997.

Eisner, Will. *Comics & Sequential Art*. Tamarac, FL: Poorhouse Press, 1985.
Gertler, Nat, ed. *PANEL ONE: Comics Scripts by Top Writers*. Thousand Oaks, CA: About Comics, 2002.
Gertler, Nat, ed. *PANEL TWO: More Comics Scripts by Top Writers*. Thousand Oaks, CA: About Comics, 2005.
O'Neil, Dennis. *The DC Comics Guide to Writing Comics*. New York, NY: Watson-Guptill Publications, 2001.

PENCILLER

Because the publication schedules of most comic books and comic strips can be demanding (comic books are typically monthly, and newspaper strips are daily), it is often useful to split up the duties of comic production among several different artists. The typical work flow is from writer to penciller to inker to colorist, and then to the

printing press. This chapter focuses on the first visual artist in this chain, the penciller.

A penciller translates the vision of the writer—up to this point in the process expressed only in words—into visual panels on paper. The penciller will design the layout of the pages and guide the reader's eye through the story, framing action, presenting angles and perspective, and creating a sense of fluid movement, much like a movie camera. Depending on the amount of detail contained in the script, a penciller may have the freedom to bring the words on the page to life by coming up with new and creative ways to arrange the panels to enhance the impact of the story. Comics, like movies, novels, or poems, attempt to convey a certain mood and meaning to the reader. It is the role of the penciller to thoroughly communicate this information and leave out no relevant detail. Penciling is much more than simply sketching lines on the page. These lines make the story breathe, make the characters move, and draw the reader into the often elaborate, highly detailed world of the story.

A penciller essentially uses a sketchlike style to tell the story. Some artists prefer first to plot out the story from the script onto scrap paper, working out the problems of how best to tell the story visually. A penciller will often use blue pencils on large sheets of paper (usually Bristol board). The blue does not show up on black-and-white

Superman

In the very first issue of *Action Comics*, in which Superman was introduced to the world, the artist Joe Shuster decided to rearrange the layout of panels on some pages in a unique and innovative way. So instead of a comic book filled with a simple grid of squares on each page, a single panel might stretch the length of the page to show Superman leaping across tall buildings.

photocopies. Inkers will later ink the penciller's sketched lines in black, which does show up when the pages are processed.

You can sketch out a rough draft by starting with ordinary paper and simple, rough squares as panels, and make decisions on where you would like each page of the comic to end. Should each page end with its own little cliffhanger? What characters need to appear on each page? How many panels do you want on the page, and what will their shape be? When you are ready to try a final version on higher-quality paper, use rulers to create your panels and try to do as much cleaning up of your lines as possible to help the inkers. This can include tightening up the lines on your panels (making them precise, clean, and detailed) and darkening lines around your characters.

Students practice the difficult art of figure drawing in this art class. Live models are often used for life drawing classes, allowing students the opportunity to learn how to capture muscle tone, skin texture, facial expressions, and the play of light and shadow on the human body.

Education and Training

A penciller should be able to easily render human movement and forms, such as faces, hands, clothing, and architecture. You should have a very good mastery of anatomy, perspective, and composition. Look into life drawing classes to get a good grounding in figure drawing.

If you are looking to become a penciller, you will need to build a portfolio of your work. You will need to demonstrate that you can handle a variety of narrative situations and

Comic conventions are great places to network with industry professionals and share and receive feedback on your work. Mike Marts *(above left)*, editor of Marvel Comics's *X-Men* series, reviews the portfolio of one young artist hoping to break into the business at the Wizard World East's annual pop culture expo at the Philadelphia Convention Center in Philadelphia, Pennsylvania.

styles and tell a story clearly and dynamically. Among the best places to shop your work around are comic conventions, like Comic-Con, held annually in San Diego, Wizard World in Chicago, and MegaCon in Orlando. These are ideal places to meet other artists and potential editors.

When you want to submit some of your work, be sure to check out the specific submission guidelines for the

publisher with which you are hoping to work. Comic publishers will typically require finished pages, and good quality photocopies of the pages should be acceptable. Do not send inked, colored, or lettered pages if you are looking to work as a penciller. Remember that you want to highlight your strength as a penciller, not distract from it.

Be sure to have a professional attitude when you present your work. Portfolios should ideally be "clean," with no extreme violence, gore, or suggestive content, regardless of the publisher with which you are hoping to work and the typical content of its publications.

Among the most well-known and innovative pencillers in comic history are Joe Shuster *(Superman)*, Jack Kirby *(The Fantastic Four, The Incredible Hulk)*, and Harvey Kurtzman (*Mad* magazine). Much of their work is available in book collections, which are a great place to begin your study of original line art and effective layout technique.

Outlook

A penciller translates the scriptwriter's words and directions into pictures, so he or she can be considered one of the linchpins of the whole comic production process. While some artists may have particular techniques that allow them to bypass pencils and head straight to ink, most comic pages begin with the foundation of pencil lines, and that is likely to remain true well into the future.

Tommy Castillo, who works on DC's *Detective Comics* and *Legends of the Dark Knight* series, pencils a large panel featuring Batman in action above the streets of Gotham. Castillo is credited with re-imagining the character of the Riddler and making Batman a far darker and grittier figure.

Major comic book producers like Marvel and DC Comics are seeing continued success with new issues of many of their classic titles, but they are also always looking for new and edgy talent to help them remain competitive and introduce comics to new audiences. Solid, innovative pencillers will continue to be in strong demand with these publishers. Independent publishers—also known as "indies"—are also always looking for new talent to breathe fresh life into the medium.

Salary

Pencillers are typically paid on a per-page basis and can command anywhere from $1,500 to $6,000 for a thirty-page comic. Page rates can range from $40 to $80 per page if you are just starting out to $180 to $200 per page for experienced pencillers. Most pencillers are freelance. At the major comic publishers, such as Marvel and DC, artists may sometimes be hired on as "exclusive" to that publisher and may qualify for benefits. But they are not technically on staff.

FOR MORE INFORMATION

ORGANIZATIONS
MegaCon
P.O. Box 1097
Safety Harbor, FL 34695
(727) 796-5725
Web site: http://www.megaconvention.com
   MegaCon Convention, held annually in Orlando, Florida, is a great place to circulate your work and meet potential employers.

The Xeric Foundation
Comic Book Self-Publishing Grant Submissions
PMB 214
351 Pleasant Street
Northampton, MA 01060
(413) 585-0671

Web site: http://www.xericfoundation.com

The Xeric Foundation is a nonprofit corporation established by *Teenage Mutant Ninja Turtle* creator Peter A. Laird. It offers grants to self-publishing comic book creators in the United States and Canada. While the foundation does not support the artist through the entire creation process, it does help with some of the costs of production.

WEB SITES

The Comic-Con Convention

http://www.comic-con.org

"The World's Biggest Comic Convention" is held annually in San Diego, California. Recent conventions have featured appearances by Stan Lee and comic fan and film director Quentin Tarantino *(Pulp Fiction, Kill Bill)*. This is one of the best places to experience the comic culture firsthand and meet exhibitors from all over the comic spectrum.

How to Plot and Draw a Comic Page

http://www.auburn.edu/%7Ezeesila/comics.html

Nice, informal tutorial on laying out and penciling a comic page.

The Small Press Expo

http://www.spxpo.com

The Small Press Expo bills itself as the "preeminent showcase for the exhibition of independent comic books and the discovery of new creative talent." The 2005 convention featured an appearance by Harvey Pekar, of *American Splendor* fame.

The Wizard World Convention

http://www.wizarduniverse.com

The Wizard World Convention is a large comic, anime, and mer-chandise convention held in various cities around the country each year. It is a great place to meet creators and collectors of all kinds.

BOOKS

Hart, Christopher. *Drawing Cutting Edge Comics*. New York, NY: Watson-Guptill Publications, 2001.

Janson, Klaus. *The DC Comics Guide to Penciling Comics*. New York, NY: Watson-Guptill Publications, 2002.

Lee, Stan, and John Buscema. *How to Draw Comics the Marvel Way*. New York, NY: Fireside, 1984.

INKER

Inkers are next in line in the comic production process, behind the penciller. Using black ink (usually india ink) and a pen or brush, an inker draws clean, bold lines over the penciller's rough sketches. Every black line that appears on a comic page, with the exception of lettering, is drawn by the inker. Since comic books and comic strips are printed on a mass scale, they must have

In this photo, Sherwin Schwartzrock inks the panels of an *ArmorQuest* comic book. The series, created and written by Ben Avery, tells the story of a young boy, Timothy (pictured in the panel being inked), who finds his life and the life of his village threatened by dragons, and of his village's rescuer, Sol, a "Knight of the Way." Schwartzrock was encouraged to draw from an early age by his mother and taught himself by studying Marvel comics.

sharp lines that make them easy to print. An inker is responsible for the comic's "3D effect," giving forms on the page volume and identity. The inker typically adds shading, texture, and clarity to the penciller's lines, and gives the panels a more finished feeling.

Often the penciller will leave notes on the page offering direction to the inker to help ensure that the final outcome is in line with his or her original vision. The work of the inker

is generally less understood than that of the penciller, but inkers are vital to the process of producing high-quality finished work. According to artist Frank Miller, the author of the renowned comic series *Sin City* and *The Dark Knight Returns*, "It's the ink that makes the brick feel ragged, hard and cruel, the ink that makes the flesh seem warm or cold, firm or soft" (as quoted in *The DC Comics Guide to Inking Comics*).

Inkers have to be neat in their work, and at times, they may have to creatively interpret the work of the penciller. Remember that inkers are not tracers. They have some freedom to express their own preferences in the artwork, especially in areas where they may feel the pencil work does not go far enough. You will need to grasp how to work with the different styles of line work produced by different pencillers. While following the stylistic and artistic lead of the penciller, you will also need to develop your own "painterly" technique for adding light, shadow, and volume.

A comic book artist inks panels that have been laid out and penciled. Finished inked pages can be seen in the foreground. The next stage in the process would be for the inked pages to be colored by a colorist (usually a different person than the inker). A colorist will use watercolors or airbrush if the panels are to be hand-colored, or computer programs and color separation printing techniques if they are to be colored and printed electronically or mechanically.

A more recent trend in the comic industry is to ink pages with the help of a computer rather than pen and ink. Typically, the pencilled pages will be scanned into a computer at a high pixel resolution, and inking will be done using special software, like Adobe Photoshop. The original pencilled pages are not touched, and the electronically inked pages can then be sent via email to the colorist.

Among the most famous inkers is Robert Crumb, the influential underground comic artist who sprang out of the countercultural movement of the 1960s. He draws most of his comics in ink first, bypassing penciling altogether and making him an exception to the general "assembly line" comic production model. Using a sketchlike ink technique that enables him to work quickly, he has crafted a distinct and expressive style that many have tried to imitate. Another contemporary inker of note is Mike Mignola, whose *Hellboy* series (also made into a successful feature film) makes dramatic use of high-contrast lights and darks, especially thick, heavy, black ink-work.

Education and Training

Inkers should be skilled at line drawing and have an excellent awareness of shading techniques that give forms depth and volume. Inkers should be able to work with a brush and, if they are interested in working on a computer, be comfortable with digital imaging programs. Inkers are at the mid-point between penciller and colorist in the comic production

A penciled comic panel by New York artist and writer Thomas Forget appears above left. The x's that appear on the bodies of the two figures indicate to the inker that flat black ink should be applied to these areas. The same panel, now inked, appears at right.

process. As such, they should be able to work collaboratively and harmoniously with both of these artists. Differences of vision and style may arise, but an inker should bring a spirit of flexibility and compromise to the comic creation process.

As far as tools go, work with what is most comfortable for you. Some inkers prefer pens, including brush pens, while others prefer brushes of varying thickness to create different effects. Brush inking, in particular, can require the most practice and learning. Beyond mastery of the inking tools, you will need to discover and develop your own technique, whether it is a heavy use of cross-hatching or experimentation with different line weights on the page. You will want to be familiar with inking sequential (multipaneled) pages, as well as stand-alone, single panel "pin-up" pages. Inking by hand can be slow and methodical work, but it can be extremely rewarding when you view the finished product.

If you are more interested in becoming a digital inker, Adobe Photoshop is the software program of choice, and a scanner will also be a valuable tool. You will want to scan all artwork in at a high resolution (opinions differ, but many suggest 600 dots per inch), and you will want to work with the penciller to ensure the lines are clean and there are no smudges. The cleaner the pencil work is, the easier the process of digital inking. Look into taking a Photoshop course to become familiar with the finer points of using the software's multitude of tools. A personal computer will, of course, be required for digital inking. Shop around for a good deal on a new computer, or check the Web for inexpensive used models.

Outlook

Given that they are essential to the process of making comics printable, inkers have always been in high demand and will continue to be so. As long as comics are produced, there will be a need for inkers, whether of the pen-and-ink or digital variety. With the increasing popularity of independent comic titles, more and more artists are penciling

and inking their own work, and this is a preferable working model for many artists. While some inking is still done the old-fashioned way—with brush and ink—more and more inkers are turning to computers and programs like Adobe Photoshop to produce great results.

Salary

Inkers are typically paid by the page and can make any-where from $50 to $175 per page, or between $1,500 and $5,250 for a thirty-page comic book. Rates can vary by pub-lisher, and some publishers will not post their rates on their Web sites. Be sure to verify your salary before you begin work. There is often room to negotiate with the publisher about fees and salaries, especially if you have some previous work experience in the industry.

FOR MORE INFORMATION

WEB SITES
Dark Horse Submission Guidelines
http://www.darkhorse.com/company/submissions.php
> Dark Horse is one of the leading independent comic publishers, and this site features separate guidelines for writers, artists, inkers, and colorists. Among the creators that have published titles with Dark Horse are Jim Woodring, Peter Bagge, and Eddie Campbell.

DC Comics Submission Guidelines

http://www.dccomics.com/about/submissions.html
Publisher of *Identity Crisis, Batman, Superman, Green Lantern, Wonder Woman, Teen Titans*, and *Justice League of America*, among others.

Marvel Comics Submission Guidelines

http://www.marvel.com/company/subs.htm
Publisher of *Spider-Man, The X-Men, Captain America, The Fantastic Four*, and *The Avengers*.

BOOKS

Chelsea, David. *Perspective! for Comic Book Artists: How to Achieve a Professional Look in Your Artwork*. New York, NY: Watson-Guptill Publications, 1997.

Janson, Klaus. *The DC Comics Guide to Inking Comics*. New York, NY: Watson-Guptill Publications, 2003.

Martin, Gary, and Steve Rude. *The Art of Comic Book Inking*. Milwaukie, OR: Dark Horse, 1997.

Martin, Gary. *The Art of Comic Book Inking Volume 2*. Milwaukie, OR: Dark Horse, 2002.

COLORIST

Once the penciller has created the basic layout and line art, and the inker has cleanly rendered all of the lines, textures, and shading in black ink, it becomes the job of the colorist to tie up the whole presentation. Many comic readers consider the best coloring jobs to be those that do not call attention to themselves. While this may make it

A comic book artist contemplates how best to color the inked pages before him. Covering the table are colored markers that will help him work out exactly how he wants the final panels to appear and how they will be colored.

sound like an underappreciated field, Mark Chiarello, in *The DC Comics Guide to Coloring and Lettering Comics*, notes: "Coloring is now considered by many to be as important to comic books as any other aspect of the creative process. Without a good colorist, the visual punch and appeal of a comic book is in jeopardy."

As comic art and design have become more and more sophisticated over the years, the field of coloring has kept pace by gradually becoming more of a computer-based job.

Before computers came on the scene, however, colorists would choose the colors they wanted to use in the comic's panels from a very limited selection of hues. Many colorists hand-painted their pages, used watercolors or airbrush, or worked on photographed copies of the pages, making their color notes on the photographs. When photocopying machines came along, colorists were able to work on paper copies of the pages. Colorists wrote down color codes on the photocopies of the inked pages and ultimately sent them off to another person who would do the color separation.

Color separation is the process that allows for the printing of full-color images. Before printing, an image must be separated into the four basic ink colors: cyan, magenta, yellow, and black (CMYK). Each of these single-color layers is printed separately, one on top of another, resulting in a full-color image that gives the illusion of a wide and complete spectrum of color. The color separator would create the printing plates, which were usually made of metal, plastic, rubber, or paper, and were used to transfer an image to paper. The results would only be seen months later when the comics hit the stores.

In the mid-1980s, this laborious and imperfect process changed forever when paint programs on computers evolved to the point where they could be used to perform all of the coloring work, including generating the printing plates. Colorists now use personal computers and software programs like Adobe Photoshop to produce digital files called separations. These separations give the printer all the information needed to print the comic.

Education and Training

Personal computers have made breaking into the colorist field far easier and less expensive. You will need to make an initial investment in the computer and software, but this will pay off in the long term with work saved. Having access to a computer will also allow you to use the Internet to research publishers, communicate with other artists, and share your work. With so many computers on the market and so many computer makers cutting prices to compete for your purchase, you should have an easy time finding a good deal on a machine that suits your needs and interests.

Adobe Photoshop is the most popular and useful tool currently in use for the practice of coloring, and it greatly simplifies tasks that used to require a lot of time and labor. There are tutorials on the Web for using Photoshop to create your color separations, beginning with preparing the finished line art and then introducing the colors, adding highlights and other effects along the way to produce interesting light and shading. You will be surprised at how quickly you can reproduce some of the effects you see in your favorite comics.

The best colorists are those who know how to pick the colors that will most effectively help tell the story and enhance and complement the line art. With the huge number

Comic artist Carol Schwauber uses her computer to add and refine the color of a comic book panel. Computer programs like Adobe Photoshop allow artists to scan original line drawings, creating a digital version of the art that can be colored by computer. These programs allow you to create various copies of the art, each one layered upon the other. The artist decides what color he or she wants a certain part or parts of the image to be and creates a layer that features only that color. By the end, the several layers of the image will come together to give the appearance of a single full-color panel.

and range of colors now available to colorists, there would seem to be an enormous amount of knowledge and expertise to acquire. Do not be intimidated or discouraged; you will find most of what you need in the software you purchase. Programs like Photoshop, Adobe Illustrator, and Painter

come with many tutorials and lots of easily accessible information to get you started with using a wide range of color. Of course, having a basic grounding in drawing, painting, and color theory will help you become more sensitive to the effects of color on the mood and impact of artwork. It is also a good idea to learn how to use traditional illustrating tools—like pencils and ink—so that you can gain a complete understanding of all aspects of the comic process.

If you are working toward submitting your work to a publisher, you can find sample artwork on the Web that you can use for coloring. For example, Marvel Comics' Web site allows you to download coloring test pages for use in submissions. Some publishers may want to see how you handle a variety of scenes, from action sequences to more quiet and contemplative scenes, and will want to see how you convey the various moods with color. Demonstrating a good mastery of lighting technique will also help you make a strong and favorable impression.

Just as illustrators spend much of their spare time sketching in order to sharpen their skills and generate new ideas, colorists should also continuously study color and experiment with its uses, possible combinations, and effects. A thorough understanding of and experience with how color can be used to create and enhance mood, energy, and texture will go a long way toward helping you forge a successful career in the comic and animation arts.

Outlook

As with other fields in comics mentioned here, colorists will continue to be in high demand given the current and growing popularity of comics and the continued increase in independent comic production. Today, coloring is mostly done digitally. With constant changes in technology (and the availability of relatively cheap computers and software), it is a great time to become a colorist, either with an existing publisher or through publishing your own comic. Right now, you have the opportunity to learn the latest computer coloring techniques and software that even longtime coloring professionals are currently busy teaching themselves. Keeping up with the latest technological developments means staying even with, or even ahead of, the professional competition.

Salary

Colorists are typically paid by the page when working with a publisher and can make anywhere from $75 to $175 per page, or $2,250 to $5,250 for a thirty-page comic. With computers increasing the efficiency and productivity of working in the coloring field, it may be possible to achieve a higher salary more quickly than was possible when comics were laboriously hand-colored.

FOR MORE INFORMATION

WEB SITES

Adobe Resource Center: Tips and Tutorials
http://www.adobe.com/products/tips/photoshop.html
   Photoshop tutorials are available at this Adobe Web site.
http://www.adobe.com/products/tips/illustrator.html
   Illustrator tutorials are available at this Adobe Web site.

ComicColors.com
http://www.comiccolors.com/index1.html
   A helpful resource site for comic colorists.

DC Comics Submission Guidelines
http://www.dccomics.com/about/submissions.html
   The publisher of *Identity Crisis*, *Batman*, *Superman*, *Green Lantern*, *Wonder Woman*, *Teen Titans*, and *Justice League of America* posts its submission guidelines at this Web site.

Digital Cel Coloring Tutorial
http://wynd.teamanime2k.org/tutorial_celcoloring.htm
   Nicely designed digital coloring tutorial, using anime-style artwork to demonstrate how to use current versions of Photoshop.

Graphic Design Forum: Photoshop, Illustrator, and Color Scheme Tool Tutorials
http://www.steeldolphin-forums.com/htmltuts/digital_colorpart1.html
   A basic, well-illustrated digital coloring tutorial.

Marvel Comics Submission Guidelines
http://www.marvel.com/company/subs.htm
  Marvel Comics is one of the best-known comic publishers, with titles including *Spider-Man*, *The X-Men*, *Captain America*, *The Fantastic Four*, and *The Avengers*. It publishes a detailed submissions guide for aspiring contributors, available at this Web site.

BOOKS

Caputo, Tony C. *How to Self-Publish Your Own Comic Book: The Complete Resource Guide to the Business, Production, Distribution, Marketing and Promotion of Comic Books*. New York, NY: Watson-Guptill Publications, 1997.

Chiarello, Mark. *DC Comics Guide to Coloring and Lettering Comics*. New York, NY: Watson-Guptill Publications, 2004.

Tinsley, Kevin. *Digital Prepress for Comic Books: The Definitive Desktop Production Guide*. Brooklyn, NY: Stickman Graphics, 1999.

ANIMATION

In our current high-tech age, "animation" is a very broad term that encompasses numerous techniques and technologies. It can represent everything from clay animation stop-motion filmmaking *(The Nightmare Before Christmas, Wallace and Gromit)* and traditional hand-drawn 2-D animation that you see on television (like *Fairly Oddparents* or *Kim Possible*) to large-scale, big-budget, computer-animated

Nick Park *(above)* poses among cut-outs of characters who appear in his 2005 movie *Wallace & Gromit: The Curse of the Were-Rabbit*. Park first created the characters Wallace and Gromit as a film school project in the early 1980s. Park specializes in stop-motion animation, which features scale model sets and movable figures. After the figures are posed in the way a director wants, the camera films a single frame, then is shut off. The figures are then adjusted slightly to signify movement, and a new frame is shot. When viewing the finished film, all of these individual frames rush by in sequence, and the illusion of motion is created.

productions like *The Incredibles*. With the advent of personal computers and the "do-it-yourself" ethic they make possible, more and more people are getting into the animation business at all levels. From constructing animated snippets and short films in Macromedia Flash for use on your personal Web site to creating advanced 3-D lighting effects on

powerful rendering computers for films like *Ice Age*, technology is opening many creative doors and simplifying animation processes that used to be much more time-consuming only a few years ago.

But even with all of the changes that technology has brought, there are still basic roles in the animation process that have not changed since the very early days of animation. These roles range from show creator to voice-over artist, and they are crucial to producing a finished film or show. They will continue to be important for as long as people are attracted to animated productions, and the popularity of such productions only continues to rise.

CREATOR OF ANIMATED FILM OR SERIES

All of the animation you see on television and in movie theaters originates from someone's creative mind. Characters that we all know and love, from Mickey Mouse to Homer Simpson, were all born in someone's imagination and eventually found their way to the big screen or into our living rooms. If you have got a great idea for a television

Japanese filmmaker Hayao Miyazaki holds a Golden Lion statuette, awarded to him at the 2005 Venice Film Festival for Lifetime Achievement as a director of acclaimed animated films. His movies include *Princess Mononoke* (1997), *Spirited Away* (2001), and *Howl's Moving Castle* (2004). *Spirited Away* won the Academy Award in 2002 for Best Animated Feature, the first Oscar ever awarded to an anime production.

show, animated short, or feature-length film and would like to get it off the ground, you may be able to create your own animated film or series. All it takes is a good idea, high energy, and a little luck to get your idea noticed.

As the creator, you will develop the basic concept for the show, including where it is set, who the characters are, and what kind of action will take place. Often this core information

Walt Disney *(left)* crouches before storyboards that lay out the scenes of what would become the pioneering animated film *Fantasia* (1940). The two-and-a-half-hour film broke new ground by rejecting conventional storytelling and plot for several short episodes whose visuals and silent narratives were inspired by pieces of classical music that provided the soundtrack. Disney is seen here discussing the movie with composer and music critic Deems Taylor *(center)* and Leopold Stokowski, conductor of the Philadelphia Symphony Orchestra, who performed the film's score.

is known as the "show bible," the basic printed guideline for developing the show. All of this information needs to be thought through ahead of time so that everyone who works on your production—whether a cast and crew of hundreds or just you and a small team—can be on the same page.

Information in the show bible may include characters' names, their personality traits and quirks, their appearance and attitude, a description of the environment they inhabit, and possibilities for plot development. You are essentially creating an entire animated world, and that involves populating it with sights and sounds that will attract potential viewers. Don't underestimate the value of good characters in your work.

Your first goal will be to work toward a show "pitch," which is a meeting with production companies who may be interested in developing your idea into a series or film. Your goal will be to convey the essence of your idea to them as quickly and efficiently as you can. Some creators will have an entire script prepared; others will just have some characters and a setting in mind. Chances are, the more fleshed out and fully developed the materials you present, the better your chances of being offered a production deal. You will want to convey some excitement for what you have dreamed up, in a way that is clear to the listener. If you have written a complete script, be sure to provide details on story structure, dialogue, and characterization. If you want to convey your idea visually rather than in script form, you might choose to present a storyboard, which uses square panels on paper (comic book style) to illustrate the flow of the story. You might opt to create your own storyboard or work with a storyboard artist to create one.

Education and Training

Show creators come from all backgrounds, but the one thing they all have in common is a great idea that they would like to see through to production and broadcast. You will want to have familiarity with lots of different animated shows and films that you can use as points of reference for story and character development. Everything from classic *Looney Tunes* to *SpongeBob Squarepants* to *Toy Story* will educate you in what makes certain characters succeed, what kind of voice talent helps bring characters to energetic and vibrant life, and what kind of creative decisions you will need to make. You should also wade through many animated shows that you do not enjoy because often it is the knowledge of what does not work that can help you improve a production and ultimately attract viewers.

Keep in mind that you are the visionary and that your team will be looking to you for guidance when it comes time to develop the show or film. You will need to be able to manage a staff effectively, while remaining open to suggestions from your team.

Even though you will not be doing any of the actual animation, your knowledge of animation techniques and what is visually possible will prove useful. Take courses in animation basics or visit your local bookstore to check out the wealth of titles available to the aspiring show creator.

Storyboards for the animated film *Shrek* (2001) are pinned to a board at the offices of the Pacific Data Images studio in Palo Alto, California. Pacific Data Images (PDI) started as a software company that helped television stations develop network promotions, specials, and show openers. Eventually it started getting involved in music videos and movie production, contributing computer generated images (CGI) to such films as *Terminator 2* (1991), *Angels in the Outfield* (1994), and *Batman Forever* (1995). In March 1996, PDI signed a coproduction deal with DreamWorks SKG to create original computer-generated feature films, including *AntZ* (1998). In February 2000, DreamWorks acquired PDI to form PDI/DreamWorks. The newly combined company released *Shrek* in 2001. *Shrek 2* and *Madagascar* followed in 2004 and 2005, respectively.

If you are a creator who wants to write your own scripts, you will need to have basic writing skills, some knowledge of word processing software, and familiarity with the basic standard format of animation scripts. Check out books of scripts for animated films and television shows. Many of these scripts are available online. Details are very important, down to the way a certain character speaks (perhaps with an accent or regional dialect), their physical features, the clothes they wear, and the painted backgrounds they inhabit and move through. Look for a production job on a series that is already in production—this will help give you an insider's look at a studio or network and how it operates.

You may ask: How do I get a meeting with the right people to pitch my idea? Seek out the people who influence the project development decision-making. In terms of organizing your pitch, Khaki Jones, vice president of original series at Cartoon Network, noted in an interview with the authors, "I personally feel a creator should avoid over-selling the pitch. I much prefer to read through the [show] bible and discuss the overview with the creator rather than have the story acted out in front of me with music, actors, et cetera."

Outlook

With so much original animation in production for TV networks and feature films, this is a great time for show creators. Successful creator-driven shows like Cartoon Network's *Foster's Home for Imaginary Friends* and Nickelodeon's *SpongeBob Squarepants* have inspired many would-be creators to feel that they can do it, too. The importance of a strong central idea, an effective creative leader, and a supportive staff cannot be overstated. Khaki Jones points out, "These shows don't struggle for direction because the creator is there guiding them, and he has a team behind him dedicated to that vision."

Many TV networks are creating animation blocks in response to the success of the previously mentioned shows, which reach audiences young and old alike. Animation blocks are a deliberate grouping of animated shows on a TV network into a branded one- to two-hour broadcast "block." This group of shows shares a common theme or target audience and age groups. Networks are always looking for the next breakout idea. Keep in mind that with some persistence and a great concept, you might find yourself at the helm of your own production.

Salary

When an animated show is green-lit, it is standard to make thirteen episodes to determine its success. For a first time show creator, salaries tend to be fixed. For example, you may get paid approximately $10,000 per episode, which will cover all of the show creator's services. Once a show is a proven success, you can renegotiate your salary and be paid for each job you do. If you also serve as executive producer and art director on the series, then you can be paid separately for each job.

FOR MORE INFORMATION

ORGANIZATIONS

International Animated Film Society (ASIFA)–Hollywood
2114 Burbank Boulevard
Burbank, CA 91506
(818) 842-8330
Web site: http://www.asifa-hollywood.org

ASIFA-East
c/o Michael Sporn Animation
35 Bedford Street
New York, NY 10014
http://www.asifaeast.com
ASIFA is an international group that works to increase the world-wide visibility of animated film.

The Writer's Guild of America, East
555 West 57th Street, Suite 1230
New York, NY 10019
(212) 767-7800
Web site: http://www.wgaeast.org
The Writer's Guild of America is the labor union for writers working in the motion picture and television industries in the United States. It has more than 11,000 members nationwide. It is divided into two separate unions, Writer's Guild of America, East and Writer's Guild of America, West.

The Writer's Guild of America, West
7000 West Third Street

Los Angeles, CA 90048
(800) 548-4532
Web site: http://www.wga.org

WEB SITES

Animation Artist
http://www.animationartist.com
> Digital media community for animators, including information on new technologies and conventions.

Animation Insider: Animation's Homepage for News and Reviews
http://www.animationinsider.net
> Online since 1993, this is a great source for animation news and reviews.

The Library of Congress' Origins of American Animation, 1900–1921 chronological title list
http://memory.loc.gov/ammem/oahtml/oachron.html
> The Library of Congress has a permanent collection of twenty-one animated films (and two fragments), which span the years 1900 to 1921 and are available for viewing on the Web. They are a nice resource for the origins of animation.

"Life's a Pitch," by David B. Levy, president of ASIFA-East
http://www.asifa-hollywood.org/pitch.html
> This article explains some of the finer points of pitching an animation idea.

BOOKS

De Abreu, Carlos. *Opening the Doors to Hollywood: How to Sell Your Idea, Story, Screenplay, Manuscript*. New York, NY: Three Rivers Press, 1997.

Koch, Jonathan, Robert Kosberg, and Tanya Meurer Norman. *Pitching Hollywood*. Sanger, CA: Quill Driver Books, 2004.

VOICE-OVER ARTIST

If people tell you that you have a unique or distinctive voice—or, better yet, an incredible range and number of distinctive voices—and you enjoy performing, working as a voice-over artist on animation productions might be an interesting career direction for you. Voice-over artists lend their voices to the animated characters you see on television, in films, and in commercials. Among the most

Popular television and film star Amanda Bynes *(right)* records dialogue for her character, Piper Pinwheeler *(left)*, from the animated film *Robots* (2005), directed by Chris Wedge and Carlos Saldanha. Other actors and entertainers who lent their vocal talents to the film include Paula Abdul, Halle Berry, Terry Bradshaw, Mel Brooks, Drew Carey, James Earl Jones, Jay Leno, Ewan McGregor, and Robin Williams.

notable of these actors are Dan Castellaneta, who voices Homer Simpson on *The Simpsons*, and Mel Blanc, who famously voiced countless characters for the renowned *Looney Tunes* cartoons, including Daffy Duck and Bugs Bunny.

One of the very first cartoon voice artists was Walt Disney, who cast himself in the role of Mickey Mouse starting in the 1920s. This began a tradition of animators looking to their own production staff to moonlight as vocal talent on their productions. Jack Mercer, who voiced Popeye for many years, came from the ranks of the Fleischer Studios, which produced the *Popeye* cartoons. It is only in recent years that voice-over work on animated productions has widened to include well-known live-action stars, as with the *Shrek* films, which feature comedian Mike Myers, and the *Toy Story* films, which feature the Oscar-winning actor Tom Hanks.

Voices for cartoons are almost always recorded before the actual animation begins. In fact, animation is generated to synchronize with the already existing voice tracks. Animation for a popular TV series can be recorded by the entire cast at once. Some actors have the ability to do more than one role, and others only have one character in them. The actors will work from a finished script and occasionally may see a storyboard if a new character is being introduced. The director (or producer in some cases) will typically rehearse the actors and then supervise the recording session, ultimately choosing from among the many takes to create the final soundtrack.

Among the qualities that animation directors are looking for in voice-over talent are the ability to understand the personalities of the characters and provide a voice that expresses that personality; creative versatility with various different and distinct characterizations; and an ability to take direction in the studio. Having an interesting voice often might not be enough to get you a role—it is your ability to bring a character to vibrant life that will make the difference for you.

The Voice of Donald Duck

Clarence "Ducky" Nash was an American voice actor best known for his characterization of Donald Duck for Walt Disney Studios. He was among the first actors to make his living primarily doing voice-over work for animation. When Disney translated cartoons featuring Donald Duck into other languages, Nash would voice the translations, lending a consistent voice across many cultures.

Donald Duck receives a star on Hollywood's Walk of Fame on August 9, 2004. The popular Disney character turned seventy years old that year.

Education and Training

In order to get interviews with various agencies and companies looking for voice-over talent, it will help to be represented by a talent agency. Most talent agencies like to

Scott Innes *(above)* is the current voice of the cartoon characters Scooby-Doo and Scooby's sidekick Shaggy. He provides the voices for the new cartoons, video productions, and the hundreds of Scooby-Doo toys licensed each year. The original Scooby-Doo Saturday morning cartoons, called *Scooby-Doo, Where Are You?*, ran from 1969 to 1972. Don Messick provided the voice of Scooby-Doo. He also provided the voices of Boo-Boo and Ranger Smith on *Yogi Bear*, Astro and Rudi on *The Jetsons*, and Papa Smurf on *The Smurfs*. Popular radio deejay Casey Kasem originally provided the voice for Shaggy and worked on other animated series, including *Josie and the Pussycats*, *Hong Kong Phooey*, *Jabberjaw*, *The Adventures of Batman*, and *SuperFriends*.

see that you have had some form of training. This can be as simple as taking acting classes in your area, joining community theater, or getting bit parts in Hollywood productions or television dramas. This kind of preliminary experience will demonstrate that you have some knowledge and experience with the medium. Talent agencies can then help connect you with clients looking for your particular voice-over style.

You will want to work toward sending a two-minute compilation, or demo, of the various voices you do to numerous voice talent agencies. Most agencies now prefer demos on a CD, but cassettes are fine, too. If they like what they hear, they will add your demo to their database. Include a simple cover letter that includes any pertinent information, such as voice range, voice types, characters, singing ability, and languages you may speak.

You do not have to rent studio time to record a professional quality demo tape. Nowadays, you can record your demo at home. With home recording software now widely available (like Garageband for the Mac), it is relatively simple to create high-quality sound files on your own computer, without requiring a degree in computers or sound technology. Putting MP3-format versions of your recordings on a Web site can be a quick and easy process and makes it easy for agencies and other talent scouts to download your material. You will of course have to consider the potential cost of the computer and software. You can expect to pay approximately $2,000–$3,000 to have everything you need to start your home recording studio. No matter what your actual work experience, you will want your demo reel to consist of professional-sounding samples that best represent you and your vocal abilities.

If you take a more traditional approach to your demo reel, you will need to rent time in a recording studio, preferably one that is used by ad agencies. These studios are experienced with voice talent and will offer the proper sound effects and background music to make your reel sound professional. It can be costly to have a demo reel made, so track down a studio that has off-peak hours or package deals that may lower the cost. No matter what, it is important to remember that your demo tape is the potential entry point to your career as a voice actor and your calling card, so spending a little money on it is probably a good idea. It should be a short compilation that demonstrates your vocal range and variety of characters. Above all, it should hold your listeners' attention. If your reel is of bad quality, it will probably be disregarded.

If you are serious about becoming a voice actor, you will need to be available to go on many auditions, sometimes with only twenty-four-hours' notice, which is not uncommon. Auditions can happen as frequently as two to three times a day if you live in New York City or Los Angeles. You will either receive a script from your agent and perform the audition at your agent's office, or you will go to a voice casting agency and be one of twenty or so other candidates who will do a quick read from a script that is provided to you upon arrival. These auditions are recorded. The voice casting agency will then send the audition demo directly to the client for review.

Whether you have a talent agent to represent you or you have chosen to find work on your own, the key is marketing yourself. There is a lot of competition in the field, so, in order to be heard, you need to make sure you are promoting yourself effectively. It can take a long time before you get your first paying job, so be persistent.

Outlook

There are a lot of people interested in this field, so competition is fierce. But if you are determined and love the flexible work schedule, exploring your creative range, and transforming into various characters, then you are on the right track. With successful TV shows

Mel Blanc, the legendary voice behind the beloved Warner Brothers cartoon characters Bugs Bunny, Porky Pig, Daffy Duck, Tweetie, Sylvester, and Yosemite Sam, among many others, appears above. He got his start at Warner Brothers following the death of one of their voice actors. After his own death in 1989, his son, Noel, took over the voicing of many of his father's characters.

like *Family Guy* and *South Park*, and award-winning feature-length movies like *Spirited Away* and *Corpse Bride* becoming household names, there is increasing opportunity for voice artists. The wider your vocal range, the better your chance of getting lots of work. With so many new animated characters taking their place in the entertainment cosmos alongside beloved older figures, there will continue to be a wide range of entry points into the field of voice acting for animated productions.

Salary

Voice-over artists are paid by the session. A session is the time period required for recording the character's part. Voice-over work for animation falls under the jurisdiction of the Screen Actors Guild (SAG) and is subject to their agreed-upon pay scales. As of July 1, 2005, SAG rates in the United States were $648 per each recording session for the first two voices, plus 10 percent more for the third voice.

In the case of an animated series, salary is based on whether the series's workers are represented by a union or not. If a show is union, then you will be paid according to the guaranteed pay scales of SAG or the American Federation of Television and Radio Artists (AFTRA). If you are unionized, you are protected by these organizations, but you must pay dues and meet certain requirements to become a member. Because meeting the requirements to join the union may not be possible for all voice talent—especially beginners—some people choose to go nonunion. For beginning voice talent, being nonunion allows you to work for cheaper rates, which can sometimes help you land a job. As a voice talent just starting out, it is important to take any job you can get in order to build up your demo reel and résumé.

FOR MORE INFORMATION

TALENT AGENCIES AND ARTIST UNIONS

Abrams Artists Agency
9200 Sunset Boulevard, Suite 804
West Hollywood, CA 90069
(310) 859-6115
Web site: http://www.abramsartists.com

The American Federation of Television and Radio Artists (AFTRA)
Los Angeles National Office
5757 Wilshire Boulevard, 9th Floor
Los Angeles, CA 90036-3689
(323) 634-8100

AFTRA–New York National Office
260 Madison Avenue
New York, NY 10016-2401
(212) 532-0800
Web site: http://www.aftra.org
  AFTRA is a national labor union representing over 70,000 performers, journalists, and other artists working in the entertainment and news media.

Arlene Wilson Management
887 West Marietta Street, Suite N101

Atlanta, GA 30318
(404) 876-8555
Web site: http://www.arlenewilson.com/main.asp

Creative Artists Agency
9830 Wilshire Boulevard
Beverly Hills, CA 90212-1825
(310) 288-4545
Web site: http://www.caa.com

Don Buchwald & Associates, Inc.
10 East 44th Street
New York, NY 10017
(212) 867-1070
Web site: http://www.buchwald.com/v2/departments/commercial

Edge Studio's Voice Design Group
307 Seventh Avenue, Suite 1007
New York, NY 10001
(212) 868-EDGE
Web site: http://www.edgestudio.com/newtovoiceover.htm
   Online and in-studio training for anyone looking to become a
   voice-over actor. Edge Studio will help determine if your voice is
   marketable and which genres you fall into, as well as if you have
   the talent to make it in this ever-growing business.

International Creative Management, Inc. (ICM)–Beverly Hills
8942 Wilshire Boulevard
Beverly Hills, CA 90211-1934
(310) 550-4000

ICM–New York
40 West 57th Street

New York, NY 10019
(212) 556-5600
Web site: http://www.icmtalent.com/flash.html

People Store
2004 Rockledge Road, NE
Atlanta, GA 30324
(404) 874-6448
Web site: http://www.peoplestore.net/index.html

Screen Actor's Guild (SAG)–Hollywood
5757 Wilshire Boulevard
Los Angeles, CA 90036-3600
(323) 954-1600

SAG–New York
360 Madison Avenue, 12th Floor
New York, NY 10017
(212) 944-1030
Web site: http://www.sag.org
  SAG is the labor union representing film actors and voice talent in
  the United States. The guild guarantees members a minimum daily
  wage on union productions ("scale") and handles payment of
  residuals. Since 1995, the guild has also selected members for the
  Screen Actors Guild Award.

William Morris Agency–Beverly Hills
One William Morris Place
Beverly Hills, CA 90212

William Morris Agency–New York
1325 Avenue of the Americas
New York, NY 10019
Web site: http://www.wma.com

RECORDING STUDIOS/FOREIGN LANGUAGE DUBS OF ANIME FILMS

A.D. Vision, Inc.
5750 Bintliff Drive, Suite 210
Houston, TX 77036
Web site: http://www.advfilms.com
> A.D. Vision's Anime Network is America's first and only television network dedicated to bringing anime to cable audiences twenty-four hours a day. The company is the number one producer and distributor of anime in North America and also publishes graphic novels and a monthly anime and manga magazine.

New Generation Pictures
449 South Beverly Drive, Suite #211
Beverly Hills, CA 90212
(310) 277-7563
Web site: http://www.newgpictures.com/film
> Media production company that translates film, television, and video productions between English and Japanese.

The Ocean Group
1758 West Second Avenue
Vancouver, BC, Canada V67-1H6
> Media production company and animation recording studio.

WEB SITES

The Annie Awards
http://www.annieawards.com
> The Annie Awards honor excellence in the field of animation and have categories for individual achievement in voice acting in an Animated Feature Production and Voice Acting in an Animated Television Production.

POV Online: Cartoon Voices

http://povonline.com/cols/COL101.htm

A great article that explores what voice-over actors do and the history of the art.

ProTools Home Recording software

http://www.digidesign.com

Stars & Sites: Voice Talent Forum

http://www.starsnsites.com

Includes links to other voice acting resources on the Internet.

VoiceBank.net

http://www.voicebank.net

A service that allows advertising agencies, talent agencies, casting directors, and production houses to send and receive daily voice-over auditions and production audio. Also offers a complete list of agencies and the voice-over actors they represent, voice demo reels, contact information, and links.

BOOKS

Alburger, James. *The Art of Voice Acting: The Craft and Business of Performing for Voice-Over*. Burlington, MA: Focal Press, 2002.

Apple, Teri. *Making Money in Voice-Overs: Winning Strategies to a Successful Career in Commercials, Cartoons, and Radio*. Los Angeles, CA: Lone Eagle Publishing Company, LLC, 1999.

Clark, Elaine A. *There's Money Where Your Mouth Is: An Insider's Guide to a Career in Voice-Overs*. New York, NY: Back Stage Books, 2000.

Hogan, Harlan. *VO: Tales and Techniques of a Voice-Over Actor*. New York, NY: Allworth Press, 2002.

Lewis, Pamela. *Talking Funny for Money: An Introduction to the Cartoon/Character/Looping Areas of Voice-Overs*. New York, NY: Applause Theatre & Cinema Books, 2003.

ANIMATOR

Animators are typically the kind of people who, from a very young age, want to be more than a passive viewer. They want to get deeply involved in what they see on-screen. They don't just take the moving images for granted—they are curious about what makes those figures move. They might doodle

on any surface available and try to copy the characters they see in animated productions.

There are many kinds of animation to choose from. Most of us are familiar with two-dimensional, cel-based animation, such as that featured in *The Flintstones* and *The Simpsons*. A cel is essentially a single still shot of action that, when viewed in sequence with thousands of other cels—like a flip book—generate the illusion of moving figures and action. Two-dimensional animation typically uses "flat" materials, like paper or paintings, as the medium. The process can be labor-intensive and use a lot of materials to generate the finished product. Software like Macromedia Flash has become an increasingly popular digital tool for creating 2-D animation, and current animated TV series like *Mucha Lucha* and *Harvey Birdman, Attorney at Law* use them extensively. Most 3-D animation is now done on a computer, with Claymation—the practice of doing stop-motion animation with plasticine figures—being an important and popular exception. Films like *Toy Story* and TV shows like *Jimmy Neutron* are animated in 3-D on computers, and this has become an increasingly popular format in the last decade.

While computers have certainly made it easier for many kinds of animators to begin producing their own work, aspiring animators should not forget the importance of a basic training in art, including solid drawing and composition

A great way to become an accomplished animator is to first become an accomplished drawer. Always carry a sketchpad and make quick character and figure studies while riding the bus, sitting in a mall food court, or sunbathing in a park. Outdoor sketching will also help you master the difficult art of backgrounds and landscape scenery.

skills. Along with this grounding in the basic concepts of art, a good sense of timing will help you. Whatever the materials used, animators must effectively manage the number of frames per second. All of the action must be timed to fit the sound, and this requires careful planning ahead of time to ensure that dialogue and sound effects are measured in seconds. As you can see, animators must have an excellent attention to detail.

First and foremost, an animator's most important pre-requisite is an unquenchable passion for the medium. According to animator Alex Orrelle, who has worked on several Pixar films, including *The Incredibles* and *Finding Nemo*, "You have to love animation, love talking about it, and understand what makes it so appealing," as quoted in an interview with Animation Arena.

Education and Training

While a degree in art can be helpful when trying to break into the animation field, it is not absolutely necessary. Excellent drawing skills will be among your greatest assets, so look into life drawing classes or seek out books that introduce you to the basic concepts behind drawing. Particularly useful will be a good understanding of how figures can be made to convincingly appear to be moving through space. Go to the park and draw people you see there, or head to the city zoo and draw the animals. Do *a lot* of drawing during your free time, while watching TV, riding the bus, or waiting for class to start. Drawing is a great way to unwind and creatively re-energize after a long day at school or after finishing your homework.

Understand the process of cel animation in and out. Learn about stop-motion and Claymation and how it works. Make "home movies" on your personal computer. Show your work to friends and other animators, and be open to their suggestions. A personal Web site is a great way to share your work—all you need is a computer, an Internet connection, and some Web space available through your Internet service provider.

You will ultimately want to develop a demo reel to send around to potential employers, preferably on a DVD. Be willing to network on the Internet or at conventions and to work your way up the ladder once you get a foot in the door. Be polite but persistent when shopping your work around to potential employers.

Show an employer what you are good at. Get a feel for what your particular skill is and develop it as much as you can. Do not try to be a "jack of all trades." Today's animation process is highly specialized, so focus on what you are talented at, be it character design, 3-D modeling, or shading. Keep it simple: if you love the art of animating, emphasize the character's movements, and don't distract from your basic talent with a lot of showy effects that might dazzle but also get in the way of clean storytelling.

Purchasing a personal computer and software like Macromedia Flash, Final-Cut Pro, Adobe After Effects, and Pro Tools may be a great way to introduce yourself to some of the complexities of the animation process, even on a basic and introductory level. Have a very good understanding of Adobe Photoshop, as it can be a great entry point for using more complex software. Look into animation courses in your area, as well as basic computer classes.

Using a lightbox, a cartoonist makes a preliminary sketch for a Russian feature-length cartoon entitled *Dobrynya Nikitich and Zmey Gorynych*, filmed in St. Petersburg, Russia, at the Melnitsa Studio. The animated film tells the Russian epic of the hero-knight Dobrynya Nikitich, who kills the three-headed fire-breathing dragon known as Zmey Gorynych. The movie premiered in 2006.

You will want to acquire a drawing tablet, like a Wacom tablet. A Wacom tablet is a flat square of plastic that plugs into a computer. Using a cordless pen, artists "write" on the tablet. Everything that is written or drawn on the tablet appears onscreen and can be saved in an electronic file. The pen can allow you to determine the widths of your drawn lines and the hue and tone of the colors you choose. Wacom tablets will enable you to quickly interact with the computer and retain something of the feel of drawing on paper.

A woman uses digital animation techniques to bring 2-D images to vivid colorful life at Studio Ghibli in Tokyo, Japan. Studio Ghibli has produced some of Japan's most innovative, successful, and impressive animated films, including the Oscar-winning *Spirited Away* (2001).

Animation festivals (like the Animation Show, which tours American movie theaters semiannually) are also an excellent source of inspiration and a way to meet other animators and directors.

Outlook

Good animators will always be in high demand, although there is fierce competition in the current market. Your biggest challenge will be to get noticed, but the Internet has certainly

made it easier to distribute your own work. Most animators, even on big-budget films, tend to be freelance artists. As such, they may command higher salaries but do not share the benefits (including health insurance) of being an in-house employee. On the other hand, being a freelancer enables you to work on a wider variety of projects than you might work on otherwise and to make more contacts throughout the industry, increasing your future opportunities.

Salary

Most animators work as freelancers and are paid based on the size of the production's budget and how many other free-lancers are employed by the production company. Typically, an animator will make $1,000–$1,500 per week. Sometimes additional benefits will be offered as an incentive to work on the project. Since there is no guarantee that a show that has been worked on will be picked up or continued, there may be times when an animator is not working or is between free-lance jobs. Sometimes an animator is brought on staff and is paid a salary based on experience. The salary can range from $35,000 to $75,000 and will include benefits, such as health insurance, sick leave, and vacation days.

FOR MORE INFORMATION

ORGANIZATIONS

International Animated Film Society (ASIFA)–Hollywood
2114 Burbank Boulevard
Burbank, CA 91506
(818) 842-8330
Web site: http://www.asifa-hollywood.org

ASIFA–East
c/o Michael Sporn Animation
35 Bedford Street
New York, NY 10014
http://www.asifaeast.com
> ASIFA is an international group that works to increase the world-wide visibility of animated film. The organization's homepage (http://asifa.net) is a great forum for meeting other professionals and exchanging ideas.

DreamWorks Animation
Recruiting Department
1000 Flower Street
Glendale, CA 91201
Web site: http://www.dreamworks.com/dreamworks_home.html

Ottawa International Animation Festival
2 Daly Avenue, Suite 120
Ottawa, ON, Canada K1N 6E2
(613) 232-8769
Web site: http://www.ottawa.awn.com
> An animation film festival in which approximately 100 films are chosen to compete in a variety of categories (such as Short

Animation, Commissioned Animation, Animated Feature, Student Animation, New Media, etc.).

Pixar Animation Studios
1200 Park Avenue
Emeryville, CA 94608
(510) 752-3000
Web site: http://www.pixar.com

Turner Broadcasting System, Inc.
One CNN Center
Atlanta, GA 30303
(404) 827-1700
Web site: http://www.turner.com

The Walt Disney Company
500 South Buena Vista Street
Burbank, CA 91521
(818) 560-1000
Web site: http://disney.go.com

WEB SITES

Academy of Art University: High School Art Experience Courses
http://www.academyart.edu/programs/satcourses.asp

This Web site offers online courses for comics and animation, including comic book illustration, comic book portfolio, digital design, drawing and composition, figure drawing, 3-D modeling and animation, and video gaming.

Adobe After Effects
http://www.adobe.com/products/aftereffects/main.html

One of the leading motion graphics and visual effects software packages.

Alias Maya Personal Learning Edition: 3D Software
http://www.alias.com/eng/index.shtml

Integrated 3-D modeling, animation, effects, and rendering solution that adds to the quality and realism of 2-D graphics.

Animated Lighting: Products for Building Your Own Show—Animation Director Software
http://www.animatedlighting.com
Self-teaching tool for producing at-home animation.

Animation Arena: Animation Class
http://www.animationarena.com/animation-class.html
This site offers a list of colleges and universities that offer classes and programs that will help someone in their pursuit of a career in 2-D or 3-D animation. The list is dedicated to schools that many animation studios feel cater to technical direction and to the more artistic field of character animation.

Animation Arena: Becoming a 3D Animator and Working for Pixar
http://www.animationarena.com/working-for-pixar.html
Interview with Alex Orrelle, an animator at Pixar who has worked on *Finding Nemo* and *The Incredibles*.

Animation Arena: Getting a 3D Animation Job
http://www.animationareana.com/animation-jobs.html

Animation Arena's interview with Victor Navone, animator for Pixar who worked on *The Incredibles*
http://www.animationarena.com/pixar-the-incredibles-animator.html
Includes extremely practical and insightful career tips for breaking into the animation industry and information on the latest computer tools animators are using.

Animation Industry Database
http://www.aidb.com
A database resource for finding animation companies throughout the world.

Drawing Cartoons Theme page
http://www.cln.org/themes/cartoons.html
   Links for aspiring animators.

Final Cut Studio: Final Cut Pro
http://www.apple.com/finalcutstudio/finalcutpro
   Final Cut Pro is a powerful and precise editing tool that works with virtually any format. It offers real-time editing for digital video (DV), standard definition (SD), high definition (HD), and film.

Macromedia Flash Professional
http://www.macromedia.com/software/flash/flashpro
   Flash allows you to design and author interactive content rich with video, graphics, and animation for Web sites, presentations, or mobile content.

SOFTIMAGE: The Digital Character Software
http://www.softimage.com/Products/Xsi/v5/default.asp
   High-end digital character software from SoftImage, one of the leading 3-D software producers.

BOOKS

Blair, Preston. *Cartoon Animation* (The Collector's Series). Laguna Hills, CA: Walter Foster Publishing, 1995.

Patmore, Chris. *The Complete Animation Course: The Principles, Practice, and Techniques of Successful Animation*. Hauppauge, NY: Barron's Educational Series, 2003.

Raugust, Karen. *The Animation Business Handbook*. New York, NY: St. Martin's Press, 2004.

Whitaker, Harold, and John Halas. *Timing for Animation*. Burlington, MA: Focal Press, 2002.

Williams, Richard. *The Animator's Survival Kit: A Manual of Methods, Principles, and Formulas for Classical, Computer, Games, Stop Motion, and Internet Animators*. New York, NY: Faber & Faber, 2002.

BACKGROUND ARTIST

Background art in animation productions has often been referred to as "the hidden art." Some seasoned background artists believe that the best background artists are those whose work is so effective as background that it goes unnoticed on a conscious level. The background artist is responsible for the painting of a stage or scene that is to be used as a background for the more flashy and dynamic animated action. Backgrounds are the environments in front of which the characters operate. In the traditional 2-D animation process, thousands of individual animation cels would be photographed over a single background to create a single scene or part of a scene in an animated film. A "production" background is one actually used in a film.

Backgrounds are typically created in phases. Sometimes one person is responsible for all the steps in the background work flow, and other times it is broken out among various artists. Either way, it is important for the background artist to be familiar with all of the various phases in the background creation process because at one time or another he or she will be asked to work on each of them.

The first phase is the layout of the initial design of the background. Layouts are typically done as line drawings. These drawings are important for setting the mood and capturing the correct perspective for the scene. Next comes inking, where cleanup of the drawings happens and heavier lines are added (similar to the inking stage of comics outlined earlier in this book). This process is followed by rough color, which gets reviewed by the director. Once the background is approved, the final paint with shading is added by the background artist. This role is critical to establishing the final look and overall mood of the production.

In animated shows and films, foreground images—those involving characters and the immediate action—are created separately from the backgrounds before which they stand and speak and through which they move. Background animation offers artists a unique opportunity to create extremely lavish and detailed interiors and exotic and lush exteriors to serve as backdrops for the film's characters. This still from the animated feature *Howl's Moving Castle* (2004) vividly demonstrates just how much intricacy and detail can be poured into the background of an animated film, making the foreground art that is the focal point of the viewer's attention seem relatively basic and simple in comparison.

Background artists use traditional paints like gouache as well as airbrush to achieve their desired effects. There are 2-D and 3-D paint software programs available for use in these tasks. A graphics drawing tablet will be very useful.

Education and Training

To become a background artist, you must learn the basic principles of painting and color theory. Proficiency in software programs such as Corel Painter, After Effects, Macromedia Flash, and Photoshop will be very helpful to you, especially with so much competition in the marketplace now. You will want to have a good understanding of the layout process, which sets the initial requirements for the background scenes.

Take a class in perspective drawing and learn how to draw objects of all kinds in various atmospheric settings. Study lighting techniques used in animated and live-action films. While you may find work with a company willing to give you training, don't count on it. Through classes and hours of practice, you will largely have to train yourself and, in the process, create a great portfolio of work. Be patient about building up your portfolio and gaining experience.

Outlook

While it is a very competitive field, with more and more animation productions in process, there will continue to be a need for specialized talent like background artists.The field of animation is becoming increasingly specialized, especially with extremely complex productions like the feature-length *The Incredibles* and *Madagascar*. Productions like these can require a staff of hundreds, from multiple story-board and background artists to artists who specialize in creating digital lighting effects.

Salary

Salary is based on whatever payment method is agreed upon at the beginning of the project. Some artists like to be paid per background, which can cost approximately $75 per background. Some like to be paid per week, which on average is around $1,250. Others like to be paid per episode for a finite number of backgrounds. For example, $5,000 might be the agreed-upon amount to produce forty backgrounds. If more backgrounds are needed, the additional charge can average $50–$100 for each additional background.

FOR MORE INFORMATION

WEB SITES

Adobe After Effects
http://www.adobe.com/products/aftereffects/main.html
This program sets the standard in motion graphics and visual effects for film, video, DVD, and the Web, and provides core 2-D modeling and 3-D compositing, animation, and visual effects tools.

Adobe Photoshop
http://www.adobe.com/products/photoshop/main.html

Adobe Photoshop is the image-editing standard and provides creative tools, adaptability, and efficient editing, processing, and file-handling capabilities.

Computer Graphics World: Deep Background

http://cgw.pennnet.com/Articles/Article_Display.cfm?Section=Archiv es&Subsection=Display&ARTICLE_ID=50479
An article about how new technology helps to transform a 2-D background into a 3-D world.

Corel Painter

http://www.corel.com
Painting and illustration software that mimics the look and feel of traditional animation techniques.

Macromedia Flash

http://www.macromedia.com/software/flash/flashpro
Flash allows you to design and author interactive content that is rich with video, graphics, and animation for Web sites, presentations, or mobile content.

3D Creative Magazine interview with Julia Lundman

http://www.3dtotal.com/team/interviews/julie_lundman/lundman.asp
An interview with Julia Lundman, freelance layout/background painter/illustrator.

BOOKS

Fowler, Mike S. *Animation Background Layout: From Student to Professional.* Miramichi, NB, Canada: Fowler Cartooning Ink Publications, 2002.

DIRECTOR OF ANIMATED FILM OR SERIES

When watching the typical animated show or film, you will notice many names listed in the opening production credits. Typically, the last one listed—but perhaps the most significant to the entire production—is the director. This person is essentially the "field commander" for all of the creative work done on the animation and oversees the quality of the final product that viewers see.

Directors are responsible for planning and designing the production, from initial concept to final completion. They will interpret the script or storyboard and work to preserve the original vision of the creator or writer. They may become involved with all aspects of the project, including design, storyboards, layout, animation, and post-production. They may also provide direction on music and sound effects.

Directors should definitely have strong interpersonal, managerial, and organizational skills. They will work closely with the producer to help manage key aspects of the project. This can include helping to keep the schedule and budget for the project on track. Directors should feel comfortable speaking in front of a group and will need to smoothly guide and direct free-ranging creative meetings.

Mike Johnson, codirector with Tim Burton of the 2005 stop-motion animated feature film *Corpse Bride*, poses with some of the main figures from the film. Johnson has also worked as an animator on the stop-action features *James and the Giant Peach* and *The Nightmare Before Christmas*. The latter was also directed by Burton, who has directed live-action films as well, including *Batman* (1989), *Edward Scissorhands* (1990), *Sleepy Hollow* (1999), *Planet of the Apes* (2001), and *Charlie and the Chocolate Factory* (2005).

Directors should be highly creative, have good story-telling ability, and have a solid understanding of the animation medium. While it is not necessary to have mastered all of the technologies used in an animation production, it will be useful to have some comfort level with them in order to understand how your staff works and what challenges, solutions, and possibilities exist at each stage of the production process. A good sense of timing is also important, as much of the animation process hinges on the split-second choreographing of character movement, music, and sound effects for maximum comic or dramatic effect.

What does an animation director do from day to day? Here is a list of core tasks he or she is responsible for during the production of an animated show:

- Identify and recruit talent (including vocal talent)
- Consult on the preliminary storyboard
- Review character designs
- Review prop designs
- Oversee day-to-day activities of animators
- Review background art
- Guide everyone on staff to understand and follow your vision and get their feedback and suggestions on how best to realize that vision

An animation director can maintain an overall grasp of each stage of the movie and the special requirements and challenges each scene will present by storyboarding the entire film. This will help him or her anticipate a scene's complexity, how much time will be required to animate it, how to choreograph backgrounds with foregrounds, what vocal talent will be required, how to synchronize voices and sound effects with characters' movements, how to pace the scene properly, and what the costs of all this effort will be.

Education and Training

Solid creative abilities combined with good project management skills are the leading attributes of an animation director. Since the director will work to turn the creator's vision into a tangible, visual reality and keep all of the artists

Richard Rich

Richard Rich, who directed two animated features for Disney, *The Fox and the Hound* (1981) and *The Black Cauldron* (1985), never actually worked as an animator in his career. He joined Disney in 1972, working first in the mail room, then steadily advanced up the ladder, rising to the position of assistant animation director and ultimately director. He eventually left Disney to form his own production company, Rich Animation Studios, which produced the feature The *Swan Princess* in 1994. *The Swan Princess* was also one of the last major feature films to use the traditional ink-and-paint process, before the widespread adoption of computer animation techniques.

on track, you will be required to know as much as you can about the animation process and how it works. This includes being familiar with current technology and understanding what it makes possible visually, and how it can be used to make your process more efficient. Above all, a thorough understanding of the entire animation process will be to your benefit. Whether it is a 2-D or 3-D production, Claymation, or stop-motion, your knowledge of the medium will inform the entire production, inspire your staff members, and help you gain their confidence and trust.

You will want to have a few projects under your belt to demonstrate to prospective employers that you have both creative talent and practical project management abilities. A demo reel of your work will be handy to show potential employers. This can be a computer file on a DVD or a Web site and can be produced fairly simply with software like Macromedia Flash.

Study the work of the great animation directors past and present, like Walt Disney, Chuck Jones (of *Looney Tunes* fame), Brad Bird *(The Incredibles, Iron Giant)*, John Lasseter *(Toy Story* and *Toy Story 2)*, and Tim Burton *(The Nightmare Before Christmas, Corpse Bride)*. What differentiates their work from other, less entertaining cartoons? How did they like to work? How many animators were on staff? Be sure to stay current with the latest releases, and use the Internet to find smaller companies that are just starting up—they may provide a great place for you to get your career off the ground.

Outlook

Directors are critical to the success of the animation process, and they will always be in demand. While the animation industry can be somewhat cyclical, the last decade—driven largely by new developments in computer animation—has seen a renaissance in the industry after a very slow period in the 1970s and 1980s. With so much information on animation published on the Web and in books, it is easier than ever to get started on your own without a college degree. And with such a diversity of projects always in production, you should be able to get a foot in the door to work on a smaller production and gradually work your way up the industry ladder.

Salary

The salary of a director can vary based on a production's location and the size of its budget and crew. Experience will also impact salary. A "season" of animation for television broadcast is typically thirteen episodes, and a beginning director on a fully animated show for a thirteen-episode series can make between $2,500 and $3,500 per week. A series is typically in production for forty-eight to sixty weeks. In some cases, a director, instead of being paid weekly, will be paid by episode.

FOR MORE INFORMATION

ORGANIZATIONS

Directors Guild of America
Los Angeles Headquarters
7920 Sunset Boulevard
Los Angeles, CA 90046
(800) 421-4173
Web site: http://www.dga.org

Directors Guild of America
New York Headquarters
110 West 57th Street
New York, NY 10019
(800) 356-3754
Web site: http://www.dga.org
   The Directors Guild of America represents more than 12,000 members working in U.S. cities and abroad. Their creative work is represented in theatrical, industrial, educational, and documentary films and television, as well as videos and commercials. The guild's Web site offers up-to-date information about the latest developments in the field of filmmaking and a venue in which you can network with other directors in the industry.

Hollywood Creative Directory
5055 Wilshire Boulevard
Los Angeles, CA 90036-4396
(800) 815-0503
Web site: http://www.hcdonline.com
   The many directories that make up the Hollywood Creative Directory catalog, commonly known as "the phone books to Hollywood," offer the most comprehensive, up-to-date information available, listing the names, numbers, addresses, and current job titles of entertainment professionals from the film, television, and music industries. The directory's Web site also offers tips on how to get a job in Hollywood, and it includes current job listings.

Ottawa International Animation Festival
2 Daly Avenue, Suite 120
Ottawa, ON, Canada K1N 6E2
(613) 232-8769
Web site: http://www.ottawa.awn.com

A venue for children, high school students, undergraduates, graduates, and first-time filmmakers to show their films, discuss issues, and meet other filmmakers.

WEB SITES

Annie Awards
http://www.annieawards.com
> Honoring excellence in the field of animation, the Annie Awards are presented annually by the International Animated Film Society, ASIFA-Hollywood. The Annie Award is animation's highest honor. Award categories include Directing in an Animated Feature Production and Directing in an Animated Television Production.

Directors World: The Art, Technology, and Business of Directing
http://www.uemedia.com/CPC/directorsworld

Ideas Factory Scotland
http://scotland.ideasfactory.com/edinburgh/features/feature4.html
> Rachel Bevan Baker, creative director at Scotland's award-winning animation studio Red Kite, talks about her role as a director and her experience making animated films.

Information and tutorials on Macromedia Flash
http://www.macromedia.com/software/flash/flashpro

BOOKS

Corsaro, Sandro. *Hollywood 2D Animation: The New Flash Production Revolution*. Boston, MA: Thomson Course Technology PTR, 2004.

Raugust, Karen. *The Animation Business Handbook*. New York, NY: St. Martin's Press, 2004.

Whitaker, Harold, and John Halas. *Timing for Animation*. Burlington, MA: Focal Press, 2002.

PRODUCER OF ANIMATED FILM OR SERIES

Are you highly organized? Do you like to be in charge? Do you always have to plan ahead and try to anticipate exactly how everything is going to take place? If so, these are all excellent qualities to have if you want to be a producer of animated projects. Producers on animation projects are typically responsible for coordinating the work of writers, directors, voice talent, managers, and agents to ensure that each project stays on schedule and within budget. The producer is the glue that keeps all of the various people involved in the project connected. At any given time, a producer can be managing multiple projects. It is important that the producer gets and remains involved in every aspect of the project so that he or she is aware of any changes or issues that arise during the production process.

The various responsibilities of a show producer begin with a budget—the amount of money available for a project and an itemized list of how it will be spent. The producer needs to be able to determine the requirements of the production and how that impacts the assigned budget. To help understand what will be needed for the project, the producer will work with the show creators to familiarize himself or herself with the show script and concept. From there, the producer will hire or approve the selection of key production staff members and will negotiate contracts with voice-over talent and design personnel. Often, a producer must be resourceful to ensure that the production does not cost more than provided for by the budget.

Since most hired staff on a given project tend to be freelancers, it is important that a producer is very organized. It is the producer's job to make sure that the freelancers get added to a company's payroll and that all contracts and

John Lasseter *(center)* attends the premiere of the 2001 Disney/Pixar animated feature *Monsters, Inc.*, for which he served as executive producer. Other animated features he has produced include *Finding Nemo* (2003) and *The Incredibles* (2004). He directed *Toy Story* (1995), *A Bug's Life* (1998), *Toy Story 2* (1999), and *Cars* (2006). Michael Eisner, then chairman of Disney *(left)*, and Steve Jobs, CEO of Apple and cofounder of Pixar, flank Lasseter.

other legal documents concerning their employment are in place. Typically, numerous freelancers work on any given project, and it will be critical that their workload and schedules are managed appropriately. Other responsibilities for the producer may include researching materials that can be used in the show and obtaining legal clearance for use of certain music or sound effects.

Education and Training

Here are some of the basic skills you should possess and develop as an animation producer:

- Excellent management and team-building skills
- Ability to forecast, oversee, and manage small and large budgets
- Excellent oral and written communication skills
- Ability to quickly identify and assess problems and find effective solutions
- Creative instincts
- Ability to negotiate
- Ability to work well under pressure
- Ability to manage a large volume of multiple assignments and tasks, while working under intense deadline pressure and tight budgets

Most of the above skills cannot be taught. You either have what it takes or you do not. On-the-job training is the best education a producer can receive. Here are a few things that you can do if you are interested in following this career path:

- Get an internship at a larger company where you can get a feel for all the tasks a producer must oversee and coordinate. Most internships are unpaid, but the effort is well worth it for the invaluable practical experience and professional contacts you can gain. Also, a lot of companies accept only interns who are currently in college and enrolled in a credited course related to the field. You should contact the company you are interested in working for because exceptions may be able to be made.

- Learn as much as you can about the work of a producer in advance. Talk to other experienced producers or people who work at the company to which you are applying.
- Accept an entry-level position in a department in which there is opportunity to work your way up the ladder.
- Seek out specialized courses in project management. These courses are usually about a month long and will help provide you with the various skills necessary to be a qualified producer.
- Research software applications that can help you become as efficient as possible in managing projects. Among the basic tools you will want to get acquainted with are Microsoft Word, Microsoft Excel (a spreadsheet program), and budgeting tools like Showbiz and Movie Magic.

Having good people skills is a must for a successful producer. A producer must often network with people in order to strike deals and raise funds. He or she must also hold creative, administrative, and budgetary meetings, in which many different kinds of people must be kept focused on the agenda at hand and are asked to report on and account for the responsibilities delegated to them. A producer must get the best out of the creative and financial teams he or she has assembled, motivating them, respecting them, listening to them, responding to them, and inspiring them.

Outlook

The highest demand for producer jobs is in Los Angeles and New York, but there is still work to be found in local or regional television studios, animation studios, film production companies, and independent companies. Other places to explore are Vancouver, British Columbia, Canada, which has various animation studios, and Atlanta, Georgia, which is the home of Turner Broadcasting, the parent company of the Cartoon Network.

Salary

Salaries vary based on the city or region you live in, but an average yearly salary range for an animation producer is $35,000–$80,000. Salaries are also based on the size of companies and their projects. If you are working in New York or Los Angeles, the salaries will be higher than those of smaller studios and companies elsewhere in the country. This is due partly to the higher cost of living in these two media capitals and the larger companies' desire to lure the most talented applicants available.

FOR MORE INFORMATION

ORGANIZATIONS
Animation World Network, Inc.
6525 Sunset Boulevard, Garden Suite 10
Hollywood, CA 90028
(323) 606-4200
Web site: http://www.awn.com
   A great source for animation news and career resources.

MTV Networks
1515 Broadway
New York, NY 10036
(212) 258-8000
Web site: http://www.mtv.com
   MTV Networks is the parent company of many networks that air animated series, such as Comedy Central, Nickelodeon, and Spike

TV. A database of job openings that can help you in your job search can be found at: https://jobhuntweb.viacom.com.

Turner Broadcasting System, Inc.
One CNN Center
Atlanta, GA 30303
(404) 827-1700
Web site: http://www.turner.com

WEB SITES

Entertainmentcareers.net
http://www.entertainmentcareers.net
Jobs, internships, and career information related to the entertainment industry.

Movie Magic Budgeting
http://www.scriptdude.com/mmbudgeting.html
A leading film and television budgeting tool used by animation producers.

Showbiz Budgeting and Actualization
http://www.media-services.com/store/software_detail.aspx?
iCategory=2&iProductCatalogID=251
Budgeting and actualization software for film, television, and commercials.

BOOKS

Raugust, Karen. *The Animation Business Handbook*. New York, NY: St. Martin's Press, 2004.

Riedl, Sue. *Career Diary of an Animation Producer: Thirty Days Behind the Scenes with a Professional*. Washington, DC: GGC Publishing, 2003.

Winder, Catherine, and Zahra Dowlatabadi. *Producing Animation*. Burlington, MA: Focal Press, 2001.

MANGA

If you are interested in comics, then you are probably familiar with the term "manga." Manga literally means "entertaining visual" in Japanese, but it has come to refer to a print comic style that is native to Japan and is growing increasingly popular in America. It should not be confused with "anime," which is a term for Japanese animated cartoons (though anime does share much of the visual style of manga).

Manga represents the fastest-growing segment of the comic publishing industry, with sales in the United States at around $120 million in 2004. In Japan, manga's popularity has elevated its top-selling creators—like Osamu Tezuka, creator of *Astro Boy* and considered to be the father of modern manga—to celebrity status on par with movie stars in the United States. According to the Japan External Trade Organization, manga accounted for nearly 40 percent of all publications sold in Japan in 2004. It is estimated that anime makes up 60 percent of all broadcast animation across the world.

Manga art tends to be very stylized and cinematic, with story lines that range from action to fantasy to romance, depending largely on the age and sensibilities of the target audience. It is characterized by a strong line and careful attention to minute detail. Among the earmarks of the style are the large eyes of the characters, a trend that began with *Astro Boy* in the 1960s and continues to this day. Some of the titles aimed at adults, like Rumiko Takahashi's *Inuyasha*, tend to be more violent. Some have been made into movies and TV series, like *Cowboy Bebop*. The comics are usually printed in black and white and on lower-quality newsprint. In Japanese, they are read right to left, and an increasing number of English translations maintain this right-to-left presentation.

A few of the thousands of popular manga titles currently in print appear above. Manga is highly respected in Japan as both art and pop literature. In recent years, it has been translated into many languages and sold worldwide. It has slowly begun to make inroads into the North American marketplace, and its characteristic visual and narrative styles have begun to influence a new generation of North American comic artists.

Manga magazines are distinctive in that they tend to be printed like novels—small, thick volumes that are roughly one-third the dimension of the average American comic book. These volumes are usually digests, or collections, of manga that have been serialized weekly in manga magazines and are also known as graphic novels. In 2002,

TOKYOPOP, one of the leading publishers of manga in the United States, tried to generate even more interest in the form among American readers by dropping the price of its graphic novels from $15 to $9.99, while also seeking greater distribution in mainstream bookstores.

Manga is most often created by a single artist, who does everything from story writing to penciling to inking. American comics, by contrast, tend to be produced by an assembly line–like team, are printed in color, and have a more magazine-like appearance. The best-selling American comics, like *Spider-Man* and *The X-Men*, tend to be super-hero titles. While the personalities of superheros in these American comics have become much more complex over the years, it could be argued that American comic producers can learn much from manga producers, in terms of visual experimentation, creative character development, and psy-chological depth.

11

MANGA LETTERING AND RETOUCH ARTIST

When Japanese manga magazines are translated into English language editions, there are a number of steps involved. First, the text has to be translated. If the manga will be read from left to right (instead of the right-to-left standard in Japan), the panels will need to be re-ordered. The art must be re-lettered and retouched to accommodate any changes that the translation has made necessary. Very often, written sound effects are used in manga and are integrated into the page panel designs. Because the way sounds (such as "crack" and "crunch") are formulated as words differs from language to language and country to country, these, too, must be translated. All of these changes can require a complete reworking of the panels. If the manga will read from right to left, as in the Japanese original, there will be less work involved for the artist, but the text will still need to be translated and re-lettered, including the sound effects. If you have a real passion for manga art and have an interest in making a contribution to the medium, you may be interested in becoming a lettering and retouch artist.

Americans read from left to right, the opposite of the way Japanese manga is written. Some manga creators, like Akira Toriyama, creator of *Dragonball*, have strictly required that their manga be presented to American audiences "unflopped," or in the original right-to-left format. Manga publisher TOKYOPOP currently presents all of its translated manga "unflopped," not only because it satisfies creators and fans, but because it also cuts costs and preserves the original's authenticity. Among TOKYOPOP's most well-known translated titles are *Cowboy Bebop* and *Love Hina*.

Letterers will receive a translated all-text script and fill in the blank word balloons of the panels with English characters. Lettering of translated manga can be accomplished on a computer with a Wacom tablet and software like Adobe

Stuart Levy, CEO of TOKYOPOP, Inc., sits for an interview with the Associated Press in October 2005. TOKYOPOP is often credited with popularizing manga in the United States, mainly by licensing and publishing inexpensive translations of Japanese manga (as well as anime and novels) and making them more accessible to North American readers. TOKYOPOP will often change setting and localities in the translated manga to make it more North American–friendly, while also inserting bits of American slang and jokes. In order to save money and keep selling prices low, TOKYOPOP, which is headquartered in Los Angeles, California, doesn't translate sound effects or flip the pages to a left-to-right format.

Illustrator, for example. There are a variety of fonts available to you, but you are also free to create your own. Hand-lettering is still done occasionally, but it is performed much more quickly, cheaply, and efficiently on a computer with Photoshop or Quark programs.

Retouching left-to-right formatted work is a more hands-on process and can require the use of a lightbox and X-acto knife to literally cut and paste pieces of the original artwork and merge them with an English sound effect on the page. Some of the original artwork may need to be totally redrawn by hand. In certain cases, the retouch artist may decide to keep some of the original Japanese sound effects in the American translations.

Education and Training

You will definitely want to have an excellent working knowledge of Japanese entertainment and pop culture (not just manga) before entering the manga industry. More than likely it is your passion for manga that would make you consider this increasingly popular field, but it is still important to read widely in the medium and to watch as many anime films and shows as are available to you.

Since the majority of lettering and retouch artists in the United States work as freelancers, you will need to be self-motivated and have solid communications skills. This will help you drum up work and become a contributing member of a smoothly functioning project team once you have found work.

It will be helpful to become proficient in a number of design-related software programs, like Illustrator and Quark, in addition to Photoshop. You will find that these computer tools make it easier than ever to start retouching in the manga style. You will find countless titles in bookstores on mastering the medium's distinctive drawing style, including creating trademark facial features and figures in battle. Even if you do not draw your own original manga, it will be useful for you to be familiar with the standard techniques as you work on retouching existing artwork.

You will certainly want to have a solid groundwork in figure drawing and some knowledge of lettering fonts and how to create them. Most of all, you should have an excellent eye for detail and the ability to work well with others and within their creative parameters. Letterers and retouch artists do not call the creative shots but instead faithfully replicate the original creator's vision.

Outlook

Manga accounts for a major portion of the Japanese publishing industry, and its popularity in America continues to rise. For these reasons, there is going to be increasing demand for lettering and retouch artists to keep pace with industry growth and expansion into new markets. Nevertheless, it will always remain a competitive field in which there are fewer jobs than there are job seekers. You will want to gain as much experience as you can in order to develop your portfolio and demonstrate your talent to potential employers. Your best chance for success is to keep an eye on the medium and know who the current artists and hottest trends are.

Salary

Page rates tend to be negotiated by the job and can vary according to the publisher or the project.

FOR MORE INFORMATION

ORGANIZATIONS

Comic-Con International
P.O. Box 128458
San Diego, CA 92112-8458
(619) 491-2475
Web site: http://www.comic-con.org
> Comic-Con International is a nonprofit educational organization dedicated to creating awareness of and appreciation for comics and related popular art forms, primarily through the presentation of conventions and events that celebrate the historic and ongoing contribution of comics to art and culture.

TOKYOPOP
5900 Wilshire Boulevard, Suite 2000
Los Angeles, CA 90036-5020
(323) 692-6700
Web site: http://www.tokyopop.com
> TOKYOPOP is the leading North American publisher of manga. TOKYOPOP's "Takuhai Online" page has a special section highlighting manga creators and nicely illustrated "How-To's." TOKYOPOP's submission guidelines for manga artists can be found at: http://www.tokyopop.com/aboutus/manga_guidelines.php.

WEB SITES

About.com's "Before You Buy a Graphics Tablet" article

http://graphicssoft.about.com/od/aboutgraphics/a/graphicstablets.htm

An article that explains what a graphics tablet is and how it works, and compares features of different graphics tablets currently available.

About.com's "How to Write Your Own Manga" article

http://anime.about.com/od/manga/ht/ht072404.htm

A nice introductory article on the basics of writing manga, including step-by-step suggestions and helpful tips.

Adobe Illustrator Tips and Tutorials page

http://www.adobe.com/products/tips/illustrator.html

The latest version of Adobe Illustrator is CS. Illustrator tutorials are available at this site.

Adobe Photoshop

http://www.adobe.com/products/photoshop/main.html

Adobe Photoshop is the image-editing standard and provides creative tools, adaptability, and efficient editing, processing, and file handling capabilities.

COMICON.com's ABCs with Orzechowski

http://www.comicon.com/cgi-bin/ultimatebb.cgi?ubb=get_topic&f=36&t=001693

An interview with Tom Orzechowski, one of the premier letterers in the comic business, who has worked on several influential manga titles, including *Nausicaa*, *Ghost in the Shell*, and *Ghost in the Shell 2*.

The Japan Comic Market FAQ: A Gaijin's Guide to Comike

http://www.benher.org/FAQ_CM.php

A guide to Japan's largest comic convention held annually in Tokyo, Japan. Over a quarter-million people attend the convention during its three days. This FAQ is designed for "Gai-jin," or non-Japanese-speaking foreigners, to understand.

Quark XPress

http://www.quark.com/products/xpress

The latest version of QuarkXPress, a powerful layout and design tool, is 6.5. You will find tutorials and discussion forums on the Quark Web site.

WellredPress' "Retouching Manga for the USA" page

http://wellredpress.com/Manga/Manga%20-%20Reviews/interview_susielee.htm

A very concise overview of the retouching process, by artist Susie Lee, a letterer for Studio Proteus.

BOOKS

Layman, John, and David Hutchison. *The Complete Idiot's Guide to Drawing Manga*. Indianapolis, IN: Alpha Books, 2005.

Schodt, Frederik L. *Dreamland Japan: Writings on Modern Manga*. Berkeley, CA: Stone Bridge Press, 1996.

12

EDITOR IN CHIEF OF MANGA FAN MAGAZINE

If you are passionate about manga but are not sure if you would fit in as an artist, you may want to make your contribution to the manga culture by becoming the editor of a manga fan magazine. Fan magazines, also known as "fanzines," have become increasingly popular in the United States over the last two decades and have been greatly helped along by the rise in popularity of the World Wide Web. This has enabled fans to communicate with each other more quickly than ever before.

"Fanzine" is a slang term for a magazine written by fans of a particular medium. At your local newsstand, you may find printed fanzines devoted to music, films, and many other art forms. Fanzines tend to be self-produced and self-published and are designed to give a voice to the true fans of a particular medium. Sometimes the area of interest covered by a fanzine is extremely narrow. For example, there are specialized fanzines devoted to a particular manga or anime title. Manga fanzines may feature regular columns written by the editor, reviews of new manga titles, and articles about creators and manga-related events going on around the world. Think of a manga fan magazine as a way for you to voice your opinions and meet and communicate with others who share your enthusiasm for this burgeoning medium.

As a fanzine editor, you will try to gather together insightful writing about manga, including translated Japanese content, as well as original material from U.S. artists. You should also try to include original, previously unpublished manga by artists from around the world. Readers will find it useful if you provide a list of upcoming industry events, such as anime festivals at which manga will be bought and sold. You may also want to feature fan art, in which case you will need to create submission guidelines.

Fans of the *Final Fantasy* animation series engage in a mock attack upon one of the series's monsters, Cactor, at the 2004 Anime Expo at the Anaheim Convention Center in Anaheim, California. The event is organized by the Society for the Promotion of Japanese Animation (SPJA), which seeks to draw attention not only to Japanese anime but manga as well. At conventions such as this, a fanzine editor could seek interviews with leading artists and publishers, gather promotional materials to discuss or reprint in the fanzine, and gather information that will provide fanzine readers with a preview of what is new and upcoming in the world of manga and anime.

Interviews with creators are a great way to familiarize fans with the process of creating manga. "How-to" sections that include specific career and creative suggestions and step-by-step descriptions of techniques are also a helpful offering for aspiring manga writers everywhere.

In addition to print versions, you will definitely want to create a version of your fan magazine for the Web. You will need to look into purchasing the domain name for your site (as in "www.yoursitename.com") and finding a company that will host your site at a reasonable monthly rate. A Web site will help you extend your magazine to fans all over the globe. On your fan site, you can easily create community sections, like discussion boards (also known as "bulletin boards" or "message boards"), which will help readers connect with each other. This sort of offering helps build loyalty among your readers and encourages return visits to the site.

Education and Training

Aside from a passion for manga culture, you will want to make sure you have solid writing and communication skills if you want to become an editor of a manga fan magazine. Your goal is to convey your passion for the medium and hopefully inspire other contributors and creators to do the same. Yours will be the "voice" of the magazine, and as such you will want to be able to clearly express your ideas in print, as well as to your staff.

Be sure to have a solid grounding in print publishing, from the basics of desktop publishing to the process of distributing your work to subscribers and sellers in a timely and inexpensive manner. If you want to start your own magazine, know that it could take some time to create a fan and contributor base. Learn how to keep yourself on a predetermined budget, so that you can hire staff as your magazine starts to grow and revenues increase.

Get to know the manga medium inside and out: who the current creators are, who their influences are, and who the biggest manga publishers are. It will be helpful for you to establish relationships with all of them so that you can feature them in your magazine and get advance copies of new titles to review. Remember, the publishers want to create a buzz around their titles, and your magazine could be instrumental in this. Fan magazines are often the first place fans go to read reviews about new manga, and you could become an influential tastemaker and trend spotter, based upon your fanzine's reviews, profiles, and editorial preferences.

Attend manga and anime conventions to get to know creators and other magazine publishers in the industry. This is a great way to get started with the development of your fanzine and begin learning the ins and outs of the business. Eventually, you could find yourself with your own booth at some of these important conventions, attracting a large and enthusiastic crowd of creators and fans.

Outlook

With manga sales accounting for an increasingly large share of book sales in the United States, this is a great time to get involved in manga culture. While there are some start-up costs associated with publishing a magazine, once you find an audience, the rewards will be great in terms of connecting fans with each other, making contact with creators, and being immersed in the art form you love. With manga finding a wider audience in the United States, there will be more and more opportunities to bring manga to American comic fans unfamiliar with manga titles.

Salary

Starting salaries for Manga fanzine editors are in the $30,000–$40,000 range.

FOR MORE INFORMATION

ORGANIZATIONS

Animerica
P.O. Box 77010
San Francisco, CA 94107
Web site: http://www.animerica.com
   Animerica, an anime and manga monthly, claims to be the number-one source for domestic anime and manga. It is one of the oldest American magazines reviewing manga.

TOKYOPOP
5900 Wilshire Boulevard, Suite 2000
Los Angeles, CA 90036-5020
(323) 692-6700

Web site: http://www.tokyopop.com
  TOKYOPOP is the leading North American publisher of manga. TOKYOPOP's "Takuhai Online" page has a special section high- lighting manga creators and nicely illustrated "How-To's."

VIZ Media, LLC
295 Bay Street
San Francisco, CA 94133
Web site: http://www.viz.com
  Based in San Francisco, California, VIZ is an American entertain- ment company specializing in manga and anime. It has published some of the most well-known and popular manga titles.

WEB SITES

About.com's page on personal Web sites
http://personalweb.about.com
  This page offers beginner information on personal Web site design.

Groupee.com: Online Community Service
http://www.groupee.com
  Look here to research how to set up your own online message boards or to find a vendor to host them for you.

Newtype USA: The Moving Pictures Magazine
http://www.newtype-usa.com
  Official English-language version of Japan's most popular source of information about manga.

Register.com: Grow Your Business Online
http://www.register.com/retail/index.rcmx
  You can do a domain-name search here, as well as research potential Web hosting companies for your Web site.

Shojo Beat: Manga from the Heart
http://www.shojobeat.com
>   _Shojo Beat_ is a manga magazine published in North America by
>   VIZ and is aimed at older teenagers, with titles including _Baby and
>   Me_ and _Godchild_.

Shonen Jump: The World's Most Popular Manga
http://www.shonenjump.com
>   A VIZ publication, _Shonen Jump_ is the most popular manga maga-
>   zine in Japan and America. It has played a strong role in
>   popularizing manga in the United States.

BOOKS

Gravett, Paul. _Manga: 60 Years of Japanese Comics_. New York, NY:
     Collins Design, 2004.
Schodt, Frederik L. _Manga! Manga!: The World of Japanese Comics_.
     New York, NY: Kodansha America, 1988.

GLOSSARY

blog A shortened version of "Weblog," a blog is a popular method of sharing a personal journal with a wide readership on the World Wide Web.

cel animation Invented in 1915, the cel animation process used transparent cels to allow some parts of each animation frame—such as the background—to be repeated, saving a lot of time and work.

Nowadays, cels are extremely rare in the animation process, with so much animation work being done on computers.

convention A convention is a large, organized event that gathers together representatives of an industry or product and its consumers.

demo reel A broad term for a key piece of an artist's portfolio. For animators, this can be a short animated film on a DVD used to impress a potential employer. For voice-over actors, this can be a two-minute audio recording that helps an actor land his or her first job.

gouache A type of watercolor paint that is popular with background artists on animation productions.

india ink A kind of black ink that has traditionally been used for writing and publishing and that is still used in comic book inking (and sometimes in inking on animated films).

line art Art that relies heavily on line segments to create the overall image. Line art can apply to more than just pen lines on paper; it can also apply to pen and ink and art done on computers.

MP3 A digital audio encoding format that is popular because of the small amount of space that is taken up by its files.

3-D When applied to art, 3-D (short for "three dimensional") implies that the work has a lifelike depth and volume.

INDEX

About the Authors

Sherri Glass and Jim Wentzel work at Cartoon Network, a division of Turner Broadcasting, in Atlanta, Georgia. Sherri spends her days as an online producer and has worked on various Web sites, including CartoonNetwork.com and TickleU.com. Jim is a Web developer and supports CartoonNetwork.com and AdultSwim.com. He has written comic reviews and articles for fanzines such as *Indy Magazine* and *Chunklet*. Jim and Sherri are huge fans of comics and animation, with comic and DVD collections that occupy large portions of their home.

Photo Credits

Cover © Bob Linder/AP/Wide World Photos; p. 9 © Ed Pfueller/AP/Wide World Photos; p. 12 © The Rosen Publishing Group; p. 13 © Michael J. Okoniewski/AP/Wide World Photos; p. 14 © Vincent Lerz/AP/Wide World Photos; pp. 16, 22 © Bob Rowan, Progressive Image/Corbis; p. 17 © Pablo Alcala/AP/Wide World Photos; p. 19 © Jim Mone/AP/Wide World Photos; pp. 28, 34 © Rick Smith/AP/Wide World Photos; p. 31 Bojan Brecelj/Corbis; p. 32 © Don Murrary/Getty Images; pp. 38, 40 © Dave Bartruff/Corbis; p. 39 © Ann Heisenfelt/AP/Wide World Photos; p. 43 © Thomas Forget; pp. 47, 48 © Robert Eric/Corbis Sygma; p. 51 © Charlie Riedel/AP/Wide World Photos; p. 52 Gabe Palmer/Corbis; p. 58 © Marco Ugarte/AP/Wide World Photos; pp. 60, 65 © Eric Risberg/AP/Wide World Photos; p. 61 © Domenico Stinellis/AP/Wide World Photos; pp. 62, 77 © Bettmann/Corbis; pp. 70, 71 © Blue Sky Studios/ZUMA/Corbis; p. 73 Armando Aroizoi/Corbis; p. 74 © Bill Haber/AP/Wide World Photos; pp. 84, 89 © Belinsky Yuri/ITAR-Tass/Corbis; p. 86 © Tom Stewart/Corbis; p. 90 © Tom Wagner/Corbis SABA; pp. 96, 98 © Walt Disney Pictures/ZUMA/Corbis; pp. 102, 103 Bureau L.A. Collection/Corbis; p. 105 © Sony Pictures Ent./ZUMA/Corbis; pp. 111, 113 © Frank Trapper/Corbis; p. 116 © RNT Productions/Corbis; p. 121 © Annebicque Bernard/Corbis Sygma; pp. 123, 125 © Shizuo Kambayashi/AP/Wide World Photos; pp. 131, 133 © Damian Dovarganes/AP/Wide World Photos.

Designer: Evelyn Horovicz; Editor: Elizabeth Gavril

Y – 741.5 – GLA

Glass, Sherri

Cool careers without college for people who love
manga, comics, and animation